There will be Blue Skies

By
Jo Cooper

With illustrations by Maria Ward

There will be Blue Skies by Jo Cooper
ISBN 9798878890601

First Published in 2024 by Jo Cooper

Copyright © 2024 Jo Cooper

All Rights reserved.

No part of this book may be reproduced or transmitted in any form or by any other means, electronic or mechanical, including photocopying and recording, or by any information storage and retrieval system, without the written permission of the publisher.

All and any infringements will be pursued to the extent of current copyright legislation.

Any likeness between characters in this book and people living locally is unintentional and is not meant to offend.

Acknowledgements

I wish to record my thanks to my technical experts, **Damon Corr** who advised me on matters concerning the Cowes and East Cowes Blitz on the night of the 4th and 5th May 1942. **Nigel Brooks** a retired fireman who explained the practical side of firefighting. Also, my thanks to **Barry Groves**, **Malcolm McCree** and **Jackie Ware** for their help concerning Boy Scouts during WW2. May I thank **Karen Hull** who advised me when setting maths problems for my character, and **Robert Young** who introduced me to the intricacies of setting up and riding in a horse and carriage. Finally, **Mandy Meadows,** a well-known Isle of Wight photographer who advised me on matters concerning publishing, and my husband **Robert** who read my first drafts and encouraged me throughout.

DEDICATION

This book is dedicated to **Firemen Colin Weeks and Bert Dewey,** and to **Mrs Hann** from the WVS, who lost their lives working during the blitz on East Cowes on the 4th and 5th May 1942.

THERE WILL BE BLUE SKIES
CONTENTS

Preface – The Story So Far		1
1.	Trouble	6
2.	The Interview	17
3.	Last Day	25
4.	The Scouts	38
5.	Tuesday	44
6.	Badges	53
7.	Smiles	59
8.	A Scout Whistles	69
9.	Lindy's First Day	78
10.	Reggie's First Day	89
11.	Learning at the Convent	97
12.	The History Lesson	103
13.	The Ink Blot	108
14.	Retribution	114
15.	The Plan is Put into Operation	121
16.	Showdown	127
17.	The Enrolment	133
18.	The Explosion	141
19.	Waste Not Want Not	149
20.	Being A Scout	155
21.	A Real Emergency	163
22.	The Birthday	175
23.	Training for the Fireman's Badge	184

24.	Real Fire and Real Water	191
25.	Not Another Red Sky -	198
26.	The Raid	205
27.	Bethany	212
28.	The House at Whippingham	223
29.	A Ride Home in Style	233
30.	Home	243
31.	Recovery	253
Postscript		262

Preface
The Story So Far

As we read at the end of my second book, 'Sparkles in the Navy-Blue Sky' its summer 1941 and we find Lindy's father, William was now working for the Fire Service on the Isle of Wight, stationed in Ryde. What a joy for Lindy. An arrangement was made with Cludgy and Arthur, that he would sleep in Smugglers Cottage, and Lindy would stay where she was. William's shifts would require him to go to work very early in the morning and sometimes arrive home very late, and this would possibly disturb Lindy if she was to live there too. There was a lot of work to be done to make the cottage habitable. It had no water supply; the stove was not connected and there was very little useful furniture.

Mr Bovington-Brown gave William a single bed and mattress; people at the church gave him bed linen and blankets. A bedroom was made in the room next to the kitchen. Cludgy took charge and with the help of Lindy, Reggie and Arthur it was soon cleaned and made ready for William. There were no pretty curtains, so William had to make do with the black out screen.

'I'll see what I can find in our loft,' Cludgy said. 'I may have some curtains stored in there.'

'You'll need a few candle sticks,' Arthur said. 'There is no electricity or gas here.'

'Leave that one with me,' said William. 'I'll ask at the Quays; they'll have a few candlesticks amongst all their antiques.'

'And I'll put out a plea in the village for more candles,' said Cludgy. 'I'm going to the shop to do some business: our hens were very generous this morning. I may be able to barter some eggs for a candle or two.'

'I can use my torch to see my way around for the time being,' said William. 'I won't need it much; the days are long at the moment. By the time I go to bed I may not need any extra light.'

'And for most of the time you will be with us,' said Cludgy.

'Thank you all so much. This all looks so nice and I am sure I shall sleep well here.'

All of a sudden Reggie burst through the door; he had found a wooden crate which had at one time held crockery.

'There!' he announced, and he turned the box upside down, 'this is your bedside table.'

'Well done! Thank you, Reggie,' said Cludgy. 'I think I have a small table cloth I can put over it to make it look nice.'

Lindy was working hard at her studies as she prepared for the entrance exam to go to one of the private schools on the island. There were a few, but only two solely for girls locally. Lindy preferred that.

It was decided that she should apply for one in Ryde so that she could travel there easily.

'I have a bike,' she added enthusiastically. 'I can cycle there. It won't be too hard.'

Miss Symons at Little Bridge School was happy to give her extra work, but William was advised that this would not be enough and that she should get a private tutor to help her with her studies. She had to be proficient in Arithmetic as well as English. There was a mental arithmetic test as well as a written paper. Her knowledge of the English language was tested with various questions relating to grammar. This was Lindy's favourite as she loved to write essays and stories. However, as Miss Symons told her many times, she often gets carried away with the story and forgets the correct way of putting the words and phrases onto the paper.

Money had been put aside for Lindy's education by her late mother's family. The war and her mother's death had upset that process, but it was decided to use this firstly for private tuition. An elderly lady who lived in Church Lane was chosen. Her name was Miss Caws, a retired teacher, and Lindy liked her from the start. Miss Caws enjoyed working with a pupil who worked so hard and listened to her every word.

'I correct you during one lesson,' she said one day, 'and you put what I say into practice by the next lesson.'

Lindy was confused. *I thought that is what I was meant to do!*

Life was fine for her. Her father had come to the island and she looked forward to seeing him every day. The thought of a new school thrilled her, she didn't dislike Little Bridge School, but was looking forward to the challenges that the private school would offer her. Miss Simons and Lindy got on very well, so much so that Lindy's plan was to be a teacher like her.

Reggie continued to rush around the village on his bike, however he had grown. The saddle had been put up as high as possible, but this did not prevent his knees, when seated, coming very near to his face as he cycled. Bikes were scarce, there was little hope of finding him a better one. He did borrow Lindy's sometimes, but was a little self-conscious of riding a bike that was meant for girls.

Except for his homework, he did everything as fast as he could. His chores were completed at double the speed. If he had had a good night's sleep and the blankets and sheets were still tucked in, he would slide out without disturbing the bed clothes, turn around and tuck it in again. He pumped up the pillows, put them at the top and then added the counterpane over the whole bed which covered up the sin of not airing the bed, thus doing it properly.

Auntie Bee was often suspicious owing to the speed to which he was able to do the job of making his bed. So, she took it apart and remade it which prompted Reggie to remark, 'I do like getting into a smoothed-out bed.'

When he was active, he chased around at what he considered was supersonic speed. He was only ever still when he was asleep or when he was drawing or painting. He loved sitting in the kitchen of Smugglers cottage with his pencils and paints. Although it was William's cottage where he slept, he gave permission to Reggie to use the kitchen as his art studio. Lindy too had a desk there for her homework. They did not share well, as often Reggie would mumble to himself about the piece of art work he was creating.

'I think that is the right colour,' he said to himself.

'Yes, but it needs to be a little darker. I'll add a little more black paint though,' he replied to himself.

This irritated Lindy, so she preferred to do her homework in the kitchen with Cludgy. She was not disturbed by the usual noises, of her cooking, of pans clashing as they were put on the stove, of the washing up being done at the sink, and of Cludgy beating butter and sugar with a wooden spoon around a bowl when she made one of her cakes. Then there were the smells as she opened the oven door.

Except for the air raids, life was good for them both, however the two remained friends, but Reggie got a little bored with Lindy as she was working hard for her exam to get into a private school in Ryde.

1
Trouble

Lindy stood at the sink washing up after lunch with Cludgy, when she spotted Reggie with a very solemn face walk past in the lane. Behind him was PC Rowbottom.

'Don't dawdle lad!' snapped the policeman. 'Get a move on! I haven't got all day, you know.'

Reggie reluctantly 'got a move on' and walked a little faster.

They arrived at Auntie Bee's front door.

Lindy was stunned and stood still, a tea cup in her hand dripping with soapy water.

'I wonder what's going on,' said Cludgy. She went to the door and peered through the glass. Lindy joined her.

'Something has happened,' she said. 'Has there been some bad news?'

'I don't know,' said Cludgy, 'but Reggie looked very sad, and PC Rowbottom looked very … now let me think … he looked very officious.'

'Anyway, it's none of our business Lindy. Come away and don't stare.'

Lindy lingered a little longer and watched her much loved friend walk head down through Auntie Bee's front door.

The washing up was completed, and they were just finishing putting the cutlery away when Arthur was spotted coming home.

Lindy was so preoccupied with what was happening to Reggie that she put the spoons in the knife section of the drawer and the plates where the saucers should be.

I do hope he has not had some bad news. It could be about his father as he is a soldier on active service. Or maybe his Mum has been taken ill? Lindy thought.

'Look what you are doing,' said Cludgy. 'The plates don't go there and the spoons should be in the next compartment!'

'What do you think has happened to Reggie?' Lindy asked. 'Do you think there has been a tragedy? Perhaps his parents are ill, what do you think?'

'It's silly to speculate; we'll be told all in good time,' warned Cludgy. 'Now you have study to do. What are you working on at the moment?'

'Sums!' she sighed, 'and they are long division.'

'Not my favourite,' replied Cludgy. 'As you know, I used to be housekeeper at the Quays. There were a lot of sums to do there. I had to balance the books. There was a lot of adding up and taking away, but long division was not needed so much. But if you need my help, perhaps we can work it out together.'

'Thanks, Cludgy,' Lindy said as she returned to the kitchen table and set out her work. She opened her exercise book, and started on the sums that her new teacher, Miss Caws, had given her. She picked up her green fountain pen, but she couldn't think of numbers, her mind was set on Reggie's miserable face.

Cludgy was putting away a casserole dish in the bottom of the sideboard, when Arthur came through the kitchen door and greeted his wife with a kiss on the top of her head.

'Hello,' she said. 'Do you know what is going on? PC Rowbottom brought Reggie home. He looked very sad, and the policeman looked very stern.'

Arthur beckoned Cludgy into the next room. He pushed the door to close it, but it did not close completely leaving it ajar.

Lindy put down her pen. *I shouldn't listen, it's rude. They obviously don't want me to hear,* she thought. *But it's Reggie, he is my friend, and I need to know he may need my help.*

Sitting silently and very still, she could just hear Arthur's whispered voice.

'Reggie has been playing with Michael and Raymond.'

'Weren't they the two boys who set off the flares on the beach and caused all that trouble,' said Cludgy.

'Yes, the very same boys,' said Arthur.

Lindy pricked up her ears and moved quietly towards the door.

'The three boys have been making catapults. They took them out to play with in the fields behind the bungalows opposite Michael's house in Oldstone Road. It appears that Reggie's catapult was the best, the missile he was firing went the furthest and he was the most accurate.'

'That sounds like Reggie!' said Cludgy.

'Well, all that brilliance, accuracy and expertise, has caused Reggie to smash a window in a greenhouse.'

'Oh! my goodness,' said Cludgy. 'Whose window?'

'Ah now, that is the problem!' said Arthur. 'If it had been anyone else's window, they may have been more forgiving.'

'Stop teasing me, Arthur! Whose window, was it?'

'It was PC Rowbottom's greenhouse window.'

'Oh dear!' said Cludgy. She sniggered and then she put her hand over her mouth to hide her laughter.

'The greenhouse is full of his tomatoes. He is very proud of them and comments on their progress every time I see him. They are now all covered with broken glass.'

'I wonder where they got the elastic for his catapult?' said Cludgy. 'That's very scarce at the moment. You can't get it for love nor money.'

'What are you talking about Cludgy?'

'Elastic. You need it to put between the two uprights, which is then pulled back with the stone in it before you fire it at the target.'

'I hope,' said Arthur, 'he wasn't actually firing it at the greenhouse. I pray that he was aiming it at somewhere else and he missed. Otherwise, the destruction of the greenhouse glass would have been intentional and premeditated!'

'Gosh yes, I see what you mean,' said Cludgy.

'Cludgy! Just a minute!' said Arthur in an officious way, 'how do you know how to make a catapult?'

'I made one when I was a child.'

'Really!' said Arthur. He was shocked. He had seen a different side to his wife's character.

'Yes, I was jolly good at using my catapult, I could hit a target quite far away! The local boys were quite jealous of me!'

'Well, I suppose, that is a useful skill to have. Perhaps you could fire them at the enemy planes as they fly overhead?'

The two of them laughed, and Arthur put his arms around his wife.

'You are always surprising me! An expert knitter, seamstress, chef and now a master in catapult firing. Whatever next will you tell me?'

They returned to the kitchen. 'Will Reggie get into much trouble?' asked Lindy.

During the following days, Reggie's sad face was often seen in doors peering through the window of the cottage next door. His punishment for his reckless action, was that he was not allowed to go out and had to stay at home and help around the house. It was often difficult to find him work that he could do.

Auntie Bee taught him how to make beds correctly. She had learnt during her time in service.

'When putting on the bottom sheet,' instructed Auntie Bee, 'Each corner of the mattress has to have a hospital corner.'

'So that's how you get it so smooth,' said Reggie. He was amazed that something so floppy could be smoothed out to make something so firm. The bottom sheet was pulled so tight, that it looked as though you could draw on it. *Almost like folding paper,* he thought.

Auntie Bee was not sure whether Reggie was being cheeky or serious. However, he picked up the method very quickly.

'Now, when you put on each blanket, they must have the same method of tucking them in at the foot of the bed.'

Reggie was also tasked to help with the washing. He took pride in working the mangle and enjoyed seeing the sheets and towels come out flat before hanging them on the line. He took to the work so enthusiastically that when he had finished that job, he was always soaking wet and had to change his clothes. The clothes ended up in the washing basket thus making more work for Auntie Bee.

She did give him one bit of advice. 'Try and make each job fun and interesting. A nicely made bed, for example, is more welcoming when you are tired at night. Make tidying your room into a treasure hunt; as you put things in their right place you find other things you haven't seen for a while. Those other things may bring back a memory of something that has happened. And ... of course ... you never know you may find a real treasure.'

Uncle Robert lacked imagination, as his only jobs around the house appeared to be bringing fuel for the fire and mending broken furniture. This required Reggie to watch and listen as he told him what he was doing. He didn't let him do anything, he had to just watch quietly. This too was always accompanied with a lecture on good behaviour.

Reggie enjoyed working in the garden with Arthur. He learnt all about pricking out seeds and replanting them. Arthur taught him the correct method for using a hoe, and he used his new found skill to weed between the lines of vegetables.

'Doesn't it look nice when it's done Reggie?' said Arthur. 'You have done a good job, thank you.'

Cludgy was the best one to work for. Reggie washed up and helped with the cleaning. His job in the sitting room was to remove the mats and put them over the line outside. Once the floor was clear he swept it. He loved beating the mats that were hanging over the washing line. He bashed them with as much force as he could manage and watched as the cloud of dust rose from them.

'Are you trying to kill my mats?' Cludgy asked.

'No! of course not. But I must get them properly clean!' he called back piously.

The best thing about working for Cludgy was that she usually had a homemade biscuit or a slice of cake when she thought it time for a break. She had felt that the punishment was hard, she too had broken a vase when she played with her catapult. No-one knew who broke the vase and Cludgy didn't own up. Perhaps she felt a little guilty for her crime all those years ago.

One morning Arthur took Reggie down to the beach to dig for bait for a fishing trip the next day. Reggie loved this. The excitement of finding a worm was tremendous.

They worked in silence until Reggie shouted periodically, 'Here's one!'

The two worked hard and filled the bucket up nearly to the top. As they were walking along the pathway to the lane, they spotted two boys leaning on the bridge. The cart behind them was of a substantial size and on it were newspapers, pots, pans and tins.

'Afternoon boys,' said Arthur.

'Good afternoon, sir,' said the boys.

'Are you alright?' inquired Arthur

'Yes sir,' said the taller one of the two. 'We have just taken a short cut, but didn't realise that the slope was so steep.'

'We had awful trouble controlling it as it wheeled down the hill,' said the other lad. 'We have done so well this morning collecting all this stuff. We got a big bundle of paper from the Golf Club.'

'It took all our strength Mr Sparrow, to stop it from hurtling down out of control.'

Arthur suddenly recognised the boy. 'It's Peter! Isn't it?' he said. 'My! My! Haven't you grown!'

Why do people always say that? thought Reggie. *Of course they have grown, children do.*

Arthur asked after Peter's family but Reggie was fascinated by the cart. He had seen them around the village with a donkey pulling them. But this one had a long pole at the front, with another pole crossing it forming a 'T' shape. Peter's friend was standing ready at the front to push the bar and thus get the cart up the hill. It had two large cart wheels and fixed between them was a box to take all the salvage. This had been painted a dark shade of green and on the back of it was painted '1st Little Bridge Scout Troop'.

'Gosh!' said Reggie. 'Now that is smart! Did you paint the name?'

'Oh no! Far too difficult for me to do,' said the other boy. 'It was done a long time ago, by one of the parents. Looks good, don't you think?'

'Not half!' said Reggie. 'You are going to have trouble getting that cart up the hill. It is much steeper than the one you have just come down. Would you like me to give you a hand?'

He turned to Arthur. 'May I?' he asked.

'Yes of course, I was going to suggest that.'

'Thanks, thanks so much,' said the boys.

'My name is Bill! By the way.'

'Now I suggest that Reggie will work with Bill at the front.' said Arthur, 'And Peter and I will push from behind.'

Reggie went to the front and stood behind one side of the large 'T' shaped bar. He took hold of it, and as he stood waiting for the signal to start, he became aware of just how untidy he looked next to Bill. 'What's that uniform you are wearing?' he asked.

'Oh this?' said Bill. 'I'm a scout.'

Arthur put the bucket of bait carefully on the cart, in between two piles of newspapers.

'I don't want to lose my worms,' he said. 'It took us all morning to get those.'

'Going fishing?' asked Peter. 'I like fishing. When are you going?'

'Tomorrow afternoon, the tide's in at two o'clock. Want to join us?'

'Yes please.'

'Just bring yourselves and your rods, I have plenty of bait, certainly enough for all of us.'

'Hey Bill, we're going fishing tomorrow!'

'Great!'

'Now,' said Arthur, 'Let's get this cart up the hill.'

Reggie and Bill gripped the bar in front and pushed, Arthur and Peter pushed from behind.

'I thought,' Peter said in between breaths, 'that this would make a good short cut!'

'You were wrong then!' said Arthur.

'Yep! I was wrong, I certainly won't take this route again! I'll take the long way round via the main road.'

They all needed time at the top to get their breath back. It was quite a strain.

'Thank you so much Mr Sparrow,' said Bill. 'And thank you Reggie, we couldn't have managed without you.'

Arthur picked up his bucket of bait from the cart.

'Please sir,' said Peter. 'Have you got any salvage that I can add to the cart?'

'We may have some newspapers and tin cans. Go around to the kitchen door and ask Mrs Sparrow. She's indoors.'

'Thanks,' said the boys together. Bill put down the long metal vertical rod which was attached to the front 'T' bar to support it. This kept the cart from falling forward and dropping all the salvage they had collected. Checking that it was balanced they left their truck and ran to Cludgy's kitchen door.

'I'll watch it doesn't fall,' said Arthur.

'Who were they?' asked Reggie.

'What nice young men,' said Arthur. 'Polite too.'

'I like that uniform. They look smart. I'd like a uniform like that. My dad wears a uniform.'

'I tell you what, I'll look into how you can join. It's not all work they have fun too.'

'Thanks Arthur!' said Reggie.

2
The Interview

Turned out smartly in her freshly ironed dress, clean white socks and polished shoes, Lindy walked smartly with Cludgy up the High Street in Ryde. They arrived at the Catholic Church. At the side there was a large wooden door. Cludgy rang the bell which they heard deep in the building.

As they waited Cludgy checked Lindy's hair, which had been forced into two tight plaits each secured with a ribbon.

'You look lovely Lindy,' said Cludgy.

'What do I call the nuns?'

'Sister,' replied Cludgy, as she put her ear closer to the door to hear if anyone was coming. 'If she is a mother,' Cludgy said in a quieter voice, 'she will tell you.'

Lindy was confused.

'You address her as sister or mother,' said Cludgy. 'Don't worry! You will be told, I am sure. Quiet now, I can hear someone coming.'

The door opened fully to reveal a woman dressed in black. Behind her was a long, tiled corridor.

Lindy had seen nuns around Ryde when shopping, but had never encountered one this close. She was wearing a long black outfit which ended almost to the floor and rested on her shiny black shoes. The robe was held in at the waist with a belt. On this was hanging a long chain with beads on it. Her face was surrounded by white material which was so tight it seemed to be stuck to her skin.

'How can I help you?' she said in a sweet voice. She gave Lindy a smile.

'We are here,' said Cludgy, 'to see Reverend Mother about Lindy enrolling at the school. We have just heard that she has passed her entrance exam.'

'Ah yes, we have been expecting you. What is your full name.'

Cludgy and Lindy opened their mouths and said their names at the same time. They all laughed.

'This is Lindy Elliot,' said Cludgy, 'and I am here representing her father, he is on duty as a fireman in Ryde.'

'Do come in, I will tell Reverend Mother you are here.'

'Oh! excuse me. Sister, what do I call her?' Lindy asked the nun as she turned to go. 'I do not want to be at all rude.'

'I am Sister Paul, and you call me Sister. You are going to meet Reverend Mother Victoire; you call her Reverend Mother.'

They watched as Sister Paul, despite the click clack of her shoes on the tiled floor, seemed to glide down the long corridor and turn right at the end.

'Alright pet? Nervous?' said Cludgy.

'Yes, I am a bit! ... I suppose.'

'Sister Paul sounds like a nice lady ... doesn't she?'

'Yes, very nice,' Lindy replied. *I hope they are all going to be like that,* she thought.

It seemed to take an age to walk down the long corridor which stretched out in front of them.

There were windows on the right which looked out on a very dull and shaded garden. Lindy peered through. There was a statue of a lady in a long dress in the middle.

'They are growing vegetables, I think,' she said.

Sister Paul returned. 'Follow me please,' she said. 'Reverend Mother is waiting for you.'

No-one spoke, there was complete silence. All that could be heard were Sister Paul's and Cludgy's shoes, clacking rhythmically on the tiles as they walked. Spaced out evenly hanging on the corridor wall were wide photographs of pupils seated neatly in uniform.

'Look!' said Lindy. 'How did they get all those girls in one picture?' She realised that this school was far bigger than any of the schools she had attended. She felt a bit daunted.

They turned the corner, Sister Paul knocked on the door and they waited.

'Come in,' said a disembodied voice.

The room appeared dark, there was a full-length window looking over the dark garden, but there was no sunlight shining through. Lindy and Cludgy were a little nervous. Sister Paul directed them where to sit and then left the room. Lindy's chair was quite large so when she sat back, her legs came nowhere near the floor.

The silence was unbearable. Reverend Mother finished writing and looked up.

'Good morning,' she said.

'This is Lindy Elliot, Reverend Mother,' ventured Cludgy. 'And I am here representing her father who is on duty. My name is Mrs Sparrow. Lindy's father is a fireman in Ryde. Her mother died in January 1940.'

'Thank you, Mrs Sparrow. I have all those details.'

Reverend Mother turned to Lindy and smiled. She smiled back and visibly relaxed.

'Now tell me Lindy, is that your full name or is Lindy a pet name and shortened from something else?'

'Oh no, Lindy is my full name.' She felt a little insulted.

'It's a charming name my dear, I just want to get everything right. I have never heard of Lindy as a full name before. We have lots of girls here with very elaborate and very long names.'

There was a silence as Reverend Mother wrote down her details.

'And you live in the cottages next to the church. Is that where you worship.'

'Oh yes,' said Lindy.

'Oh yes,' said Cludgy. 'We go every Sunday.'

'It's a lovely church,' continued Lindy, 'everyone is so nice.'

'You will be expected to attend the Catholic Mass on Wednesday mornings and Benediction on Friday afternoons during term time. Is that alright with you Mrs Sparrow? And do you think it will be alright with her father?'

'Yes, we know,' said Cludgy. 'Lindy's tutor who helped her with extra work for her entrance exam told me all about the school. Her name is Miss Caws.'

'I know Miss Caws, she attends services here sometimes, but her attendance has decreased lately.'

'She is rather elderly; she finds it hard to walk a distance.'

'I saw your entrance exam paper Lindy, it was excellent. Well done!'

'Thank you,' said Lindy a little surprised.

'She did work very hard,' said Cludgy. 'Miss Caws is a lovely teacher.'

'Now Lindy dear, I have arranged for one of our senior girls to take you around the school. She'll be waiting for you at the foot of the stairs.'

Lindy pushed herself from the tall chair. Cludgy noticed that she winced as her feet touched the floor.

Bother, she needs new shoes, she has grown out of those, Cludgy thought.

As Lindy left the room, she heard Reverend Mother say, 'The fees, she will have a small grant, and I understand that there is money from her mother's estate that should cover the rest.'

A wave of sadness came over Lindy as she overheard her mother referred to. She looked up and there was a girl waiting for her.

Katharine Lloyd was much older than Lindy and had badges on her jumper.

'Hello Lindy, I'm Katharine.'

'How do you do?' said Lindy.

'I'm going to show you around the school.'

'Thank you. Excuse me but may I ask what are those badges for?' asked Lindy.

'I am a prefect and a sports captain,' Katharine said. 'Come on I will give you a guided tour of this establishment.'

They walked around the school; they started in the playground.

'This is the tennis court!' she said. 'It's the correct size. We play netball and rounders here too.'

It was made of large blocks of concrete and was not nearly as good as the one that belonged to the Quays. Lindy thought it best not to mention this.

'I love tennis, I played it at my old school,' she said.

'What at Little Bridge?' Katharine was astounded.

'No, in Brighton – I left Oakleigh School in December, 1939. Gosh that is a long time ago now. There is a tennis court near where I live now and I play there with my friend Reggie.'

They walked up some steps.

'This part is called the nun's garden,' said Katharine. The area had a design laid out in flag stones with flower beds between, but thousands of school girl feet, during hundreds of playtimes, had stamped down any signs of plant life.

'Not much like a garden, is it?' said Katharine. 'And this is the walnut tree.'

The two girls stood and looked up. 'Looks healthy doesn't it,' said Katharine, 'but I have never had a good walnut from it.'

Lindy was shown the main hall where assemblies took place, the cloak room where she was to leave her coat and the lavatories. They could not go into the class room that would be hers when she attended the school in September as there was a lesson going on.

They returned to Reverend Mother's sitting room and after knocking, the two girls went in.

'Thank you, Katharine,' said Reverend Mother, 'you may return to your class now.'

'Thank you, Katharine,' said Lindy.

From the depths of her robe, Reverend Mother put her hand into her pocket and took out a key. She crossed the room and opened the door of the sideboard. Inside and packed neatly were folded shirts, gymslips, ties and hats.

'Help yourself Lindy,' she said.

'I know I promised you a new uniform Lindy,' said Cludgy, 'but you need new shoes. We have to sort that problem out first. Any money will have to go towards those. But don't worry, I'll make sure your uniform is smart and you will look your best.'

3
Last Day

Reggie had finished his days of punishment for breaking PC Rowbottom's window. Surprisingly he had enjoyed most of it. He had learnt many skills from Arthur, had fun doing the washing with Auntie Bee and enjoyed the cakes and biscuits from Cludgy. He did a lot of daydreaming with Uncle Robert, who often forgot that Reggie was there. One day Uncle Robert fell asleep, so Reggie found a piece of paper and a pencil and sketched him.

'I wonder what we will be doing today?' said Reggie as the two friends walked around the lane.

'I don't know.' said Lindy.

'Surely, Miss Simons won't want us to learn anything,' he said. 'It's all too late for that, we have chosen our schools. You don't have to prove how clever you are, you have already got into your senior school.'

'I wish you wouldn't say that!' said Lindy. 'I'm not clever. I just work hard. **You** don't concentrate unless you are drawing or painting something.'

'That's why I am going to a school that has lots of art. They also teach woodwork and other practical things. I won't have to do any more sums. Whoopee!'

'Wait a minute Reggie, won't you have to measure things when you are putting pieces of wood together?

That's using maths, and adding up and taking away. You will be measuring angles and shapes!'

'Oh yeah, I hadn't thought of that.' Reggie paused. 'But then there will be a point to the maths, instead of just a load of numbers on the blackboard.'

'True!' said Lindy. 'True! See, so you are clever! You would be surprised just how clever you really are if you applied yourself a bit more!'

'You sound just like Auntie Bee and my Mum. That's what they say.'

'Well do you think that your Mum and Auntie Bee are clever?'

'Oh yeah, ...very.'

'Well, they must be right then!'

The playground was full of noise from excited children when they arrived. There was a football game taking place. Two piles of jumpers made up the goal posts which were placed apart at the exact distance for the game. This was in front of the school's vegetable plot. Reggie joined that group, and proceeded to dominate the game, scoring a goal within a few minutes of starting to play.

Lindy stood leaning against the wall by the three steps which led up to the main front door of the school. She looked around her and remembered her first day in May 1940.

It was the same, but different. Reggie was playing football as he had done last year when she first met him, but he was now more obvious owing to his size. He was taller, and had developed his skills and scored another goal as she was watching. It was a magnificent powerful kick, so strong that it flew over the small wire fence, behind which was the school's allotment. The ball past the tomatoes, went through the potato patch and ended up lodged in the bamboo poles which supported the runner beans. Reggie cheered wildly, friends patted him on the back and he danced around with his arms outstretched like an aeroplane. The pupils had been banned from going into this area; the goalie was reluctant to break the rules. The game had come to a stop.

'I'll get it,' said Reggie when he realised where the ball had ended up. He went up to the back gate opposite the Methodist Church, looked left and right to check that there wasn't a teacher to stop him, and then he dropped down and crawled under the fence and along the paths to the beds where the runner beans were growing. He found the ball. It was quite high up, he had to make a decision as to whether he stood up and risked being seen, or to remain close to the ground and shake the poles. He chose the latter.

The poles shook, the ball dropped down into Reggie's hands just as the bell rang to call the children into class. Picking a runner bean and putting it into his mouth he tucked the ball under his arm, quickly retraced his steps and ran back to the playground.

Once the children were lined up and quiet Miss Simons asked, 'Did I see the runner beans shaking?'

'It was the wind,' said the rest of the team.

'Yeah, definitely the wind,' said another of the boys. 'Yeah, the wind. Can't you feel it?'

'No, I can't,' said Miss Simons. 'No, I can't. Now that is really strange.'

The teams caused a diversion by arguing over who owned which jumper that had been collected from the improvised goal posts. This allowed Reggie to put the remainder of the runner bean in his mouth. Miss Simons went over to the boys to prevent the situation developing into a fight.

The school was very proud of their allotment. In October 1939 Arthur had been involved in creating a vegetable patch for the children to work in and learn about how vegetables grow. It was part of the "Dig for Victory" campaign.

The work needed for preparing the area was hard, so the children were soon joined by locals who lived nearby. They armed themselves with spades and did most of the digging. Feeling quite part of the project they continued to come in and weed, thin out, and nurture the vegetables. Although it was the locals who looked after the allotment, the children did visit some time, and under supervision worked along-side the older gardeners.

Stood in their lines, there were groups of girls chatting excitedly. Some were moving on to new schools, others were staying. Lindy envied them, she would have preferred to stay at Little Bridge School. She had liked Miss Simons very much. She felt she was an honest teacher and marked her work fairly.

Lindy lined up with her class.

'Hello Lindy!' said one of her classmates. 'Have you got any plans for the holidays?' Lindy opened her mouth to replay, but was stopped as she continued, 'I have! I am going to the beach every day.'

'That's nice!' replied Lindy. 'I hope the weather is fine and there are not too many raids.'

Miss Simons rang the bell again. Late-comers ran into their lines. The chatter continued.

'We are not going to our class rooms until there is complete silence!' said Miss Simons

She always says the same phrase every school day. Lindy thought. *But that is the last time I shall hear that.*

Reggie still chewing the remains of his runner bean stood behind Lindy and poked her in the back. Lindy looked over her shoulder. 'What are you eating?'

'A runner bean.' said Reggie with a cheeky smile.

'You thief! You are impossible, you got that from the allotment, didn't you?'

'Yes, I did, and it's delicious.'

'You are impossible, that was stealing! And don't give me that rubbish about 'gifts from heaven above' and God won't mind!'

Reggie finished his mouthful, before they went into the class room, and stood by their desks. Children from Class Two, and their teacher Miss Framble, joined them and stood in the space at the end of the room.

Miss Simons lifted the lid of the piano, and opened her hymn book.

'It's a lovely day, and a jolly day as it is the end of term, so I chose 'All things bright and beautiful.' Those leaving today have sung this so many times, you should know all the words, however if anyone is struggling ... just join in with the chorus.'

The children sang heartily, and belted out the favourite hymn with gusto.

Prayers were said afterwards. 'Eyes shut, hands together,' she instructed the children. They obeyed.

She prayed that those leaving will be successful in life, for those staying that they have a happy holiday and return with renewed enthusiasm to work hard. Then she prayed for peace. *Everyone always prays for peace,* thought Lindy, *but will it ever come?'*

'Amen,' said Miss Simons.

'Amen,' repeated the children.

The headmistress returned to the piano to play an impromptu piece of marching music for Class Two children to return to their class room.

When the music had finished and the door closed behind them, Miss Simons returned to her desk, told the class to sit down and announced, 'Today we are going to tidy and clean up this room.'

'Bother! I thought we were going to have some fun!' said Reggie quietly under his breath but easily heard by all the pupils near him who sniggered. Miss Simons, whose face remained stern, also heard him.

'Well Reggie! If you would let me finish.' Miss Simons stared at him. Reggie looked at the floor.

'I have some activities for you all today, but we must do the work first.'

'Your desks have to be cleaned out. Throw the rubbish away, being mindful of waste paper that can be reused or sent to salvage. Your pictures on the walls need to be taken down. Since a lot of them are yours Reggie, would you like to take on that job. The inkwells need to be emptied back into the bottle, using the funnel of course and then they need to be washed until they are clean. Can I have volunteers for that?' Three hands went up. 'Thank you, Roseanna and Mary. Lindy I have another job for you to do.'

Further tasks were distributed; there was dusting, sweeping, cleaning shelves and general tidying to be done.

'Lindy, would you like to help me sort out the books? I want to put them back into some order.'

'Of course,' said Lindy.

'I know you like books, I thought you would handle them well as some of them are quite frail now.'

'What sort of order do you want?' asked Lindy.

'Well, let me think ... I want to be able to find a specific book without having to search through all the shelves. For instance, if I want to find 'Pollyanna' by Eleanor Porter, I can go to it easily.'

'You leant me that book once, when I first came,' said Lindy.

'So, I did! I remember. Did you enjoy it?'

'Oh yes, it was very good. Pollyanna was very outspoken in the book.'

'Bit like Reggie!'

'Yes, definitely like Reggie!'

'I think the best way is to sort them by the name of the author.' She picked up a copy of the book, "The Railway Children." Now this one was written by Edith Nesbit, so that one will go before Pollyanna .'

'So I'll sort them by the first letter of their surname,' said Lindy.

'Yes that's right, then you sort them again by the first and second letter of their surname.'

'I understand.' Lindy was eager to get on.

They emptied out the books onto the floor and found cloths to wipe down the shelves. Then Lindy sat happily on the floor picking up each book, opening it, reading a bit of the first page, and laying it down in alphabetical order. There was a small pile of books that were torn, some with pages missing and others that had been written on.

'What a sad pile!' said Miss Simons as she picked up one of the books from the stack in front of her. The cover fell off.

'It's all there,' said Lindy. 'Every page, there is nothing missing.'

'Ah yes, "Five Children and It;" this has been such a popular book, so many children have read it. It's by Edith Nesbit again. I don't want to throw it away; it's such a good read. I know, would you please put that and others in a similar condition, on a separate shelf, and I'll go through them later. Some maybe not worth saving and I'll send them to salvage. Others like this one, however dilapidated, must be saved.'

Lindy nicknamed the shelf for these sad and broken books, the "Casualty Department."

There was a short 15-minute break at 11 o'clock after which the pupils and Miss Simons returned to finish their work.

'My, my! Haven't you done well,' said Miss Simons. 'The classroom looks lovely, tidy and ready for next term.

The walls are bare, but will be filled with new work in the Autumn. Go outside now and have your lunch.'

The children filed out, and Reggie approached Miss Simons.

'Yes Reggie,' she said. 'How can I help you?'

'I just want to say, how much I have enjoyed being in your class.'

'That was very nice of you to say so,' said Miss Simons. She, remembering all the problems she had had with Reggie, crossed her fingers, and continued, 'I have enjoyed having you in my class.' *There was never a dull moment with Reggie,* she thought. Reggie remained rooted to the spot.

'Yes?' said Miss Simons, 'was there something else?'

'Well ... err ... Please ... I have so many pictures to take home, do you ... have you got ...'

'What are you asking for?'

'A bag to put my pictures in. I don't want to drop them on my way home.'

Miss Simons smiled. 'Leave them on my desk, I have some cardboard and string and will make them into a large flat parcel for you, so you can carry them easily.'

'Thanks, thanks very much.' Reggie said with a broad grin on his face. He rushed out of the door and looked back and said, 'Yeah thanks Miss Simons.'

After lunch, the children returned to their extra clean class room. Miss Simons said that the activity for the afternoon was to use just a piece of paper and a pencil.

The class was confused, as Miss Simons stood there with two piles of paper. 'The challenge is about your future.' The children were captivated. 'You are to draw a picture or write a story about what you would like your future to be. But you only have 45 minutes from now to finish it. Then we will have time to show your pictures and read your stories. I have two piles of paper and some pencils on my desk, come up and help yourself.'

Lindy took a lined piece of paper; Reggie took a plain one.

Lindy wrote about her father and living in Smugglers Cottage. She wrote that she wanted her dad to work in a clothes shop in Ryde, and she was going to live in Little Bridge, work hard, get her exams and become a teacher.

Reggie drew a picture of himself with his father and mother. They were sitting on a tombstone in Little Bridge church yard, their arms were around each other. There was an owl sitting on a branch above their heads.

When the 45 minutes were up, Miss Simons called out. 'Put your pencils down, time to tell everyone what your plans were going to be.

According to the children's plans there were farmers, fishermen, doctors, nurses and bizarrely one boy wrote that he was 'going to be rich.' He didn't write how he was going to do that.

Lindy read her short piece out about her father, and then it was Reggie's turn. Everyone understood the picture, but were confused about the owl.

'Why is there an owl in the picture,' asked Miss Simons.

'He is a back to front owl!' said Reggie, 'my dad told me about this bird.'

The class looked confused. 'Just what do you mean a back to front owl?' asked Miss Simons

'Shall I get up and show you?'

'Yes please, I am intrigued!'

Reggie stood up and moved to the front of the class. He put his hands tucked under his arms and began to flap them furiously. Next he walked backwards nodding his head and chanted, 'Ooo twit.'

The classroom was filled with laughter. The pupils got up found a space and joined in.

'Ooo twit, Ooo twit,' the class chanted.

From next door Miss Framble walked in to see what the commotion was. She walked over to Miss Simons.

'It's Reggie Mitchell,' said Miss Simons. She had to articulate her words and mouth the explanation. There was no point in shouting as the noise was too excessive. 'They are pretending to be back to front owls.'

Miss Framble was confused and was none the wiser.

'I think it is time they went out to play. They could do with using up some of that energy, and I could do with a cup of tea.'

When it was time to leave for the last time, Miss Simons stood at the door, shook hands and spoke to every pupil as they left the room. She knew every child so well that she was able to say something different to each one.

Standing in front of Miss Simons, Reggie put down his parcel of pictures so that he could shake hands.

'Thank you, Miss Simons,' he said. 'I'm going to work hard at my new school!'

It's a pity that you didn't work harder here, thought Miss Simons as she managed to say. 'I hope you do,' and then she added, 'I trust you will. You have many talents, Reggie Mitchell. Good Luck and keep up the good work.'

Reggie picked up his parcel again and left the classroom. He waited for Lindy and together they walked along the path from the door and through the gate for the last time. Lindy's bag was full of her work, there were a few pages of her stories that had been added to the walls, but mainly her bag was bulging with her exercise books.

'Where are you going to put all those pictures Reggie?' asked Lindy. 'Don't know! Maybe some will go on the walls of my bedroom.'

'What about putting one or two on the walls of Smugglers Cottage.'

'Of course, you choose. I must save the best ones for my dad,' said Reggie.

4
The Scouts

Reggie mingled with the congregation as they came out from the service. It had been a church parade. The scouts and the cubs had filled a lot of pews that Sunday. There were also other uniforms proudly being worn by men and women. Reggie had dressed as he usually did, he put on anything he could find. Fortunately, Auntie Bee had ironed his shirt, and did her best to brush down his favourite shorts, but that did not prevent him finding yesterday's socks and a sleeveless jumper to wear. This had got a tear in it, caused by catching it on the door handle. His socks were around his ankles, and his shoes were scuffed.

'Mr Scout Leader,' Reggie called as he waved his arm. Mr Knott turned around once he heard his name, but could not see who was calling him as it was quite busy.

'Excuse me!' said Auntie Bee. 'You should say "excuse me," and his name is Mr Knott.'

'Mr Knott, 'Scuse me! ... Mr Knott.' Reggie called again.

'Please!' Auntie Bee butted in again. 'You should say. "Excuse me please Mr Knott."'

Reggie put up his arm again and was about to call out again when Auntie Bee stopped him. 'Why don't you go up to him and speak. It's rude to shout at him.'

The scouts lined up on the grass in between the endless head stones. Mr Knott called them to stand to attention and then said, 'Well done boys you all turned out well. You all look very smart. I look forward to seeing you on Tuesday evening at the Drill Hall.'

Mr Knott then gave an incomprehensible command; they all saluted and were dismissed.

'Why doesn't he give commands that can be understood?' Reggie whispered to Auntie Bee.

'I'm sure they do understand,' she replied, 'otherwise they would not have understood what to do.'

'I suppose so!' agreed Reggie.

'Go on Reggie, Mr Knott is on his own. Go and speak to him now!' suggested Auntie Bee.

Mr Knott was tall. He was dressed in his scout leaders' uniform. It was obvious that his shorts had been ironed. The creases on each leg, front and back were as sharp as a knife. He also had sharp creases on his sleeves. His scarf was gold in colour and was hung around his neck. The ends of it had been twisted into two long sausages which hung at equal length over the front of his shirt. The two tails were held together by a leather woggle. His long legs were covered in dark green socks which finished neatly just below his knees, which peeped out below his shorts. At the end of these very long legs were very shiny shoes. Mr Knott had a brim on his hat, but Reggie couldn't see what was on top of this as he was too small.

He moved towards him. Despite his growth spurt Reggie felt extremely small in front of Mr Knott. Reggie had to tilt his head back and shade his eyes with his hand to shield them from the sun which was directly behind this very tall man.

'Excuse me Sir,' said Reggie

'Yes, young man. How can I help you?'

'You see ... err ... I helped some scouts up the hill, ... err and err ... I liked their uniform ... and err ... '

'Yes?'

'Well ... err ... I'd like to come, err ... go on Tuesday ... err ... to the drill hall.'

'Are you asking me if you can join the Scouts?'

'Yes,' said Reggie

'You are Reggie Mitchell, aren't you?' said Mr Knott.

'Yes sir, ... err ...Mr Knott sir.'

Auntie Bee was standing close by, she had never heard Reggie so nervous. He was usually confident and very outspoken.

'You've not been a cub scout?' asked Mr Knott.

'No sir! I come from Portsmouth. I never saw none of them there.'

'Any of them,' said Auntie Bee who was standing just behind him. 'You never saw any of them.'

'Yes, that's right. That's what I said, didn't I?'

Mr Knott smiled. 'I think it might be a good idea if you came a little earlier on Tuesday and it might be fortuitous to bring your Mum or Dad with you. Then I can tell you all about the Scout Movement.'

'My Dad's in the army, my Mum's in Southampton, will my Auntie Bee do?'

Mr Knott chuckled! 'Yes, Auntie Bee will do nicely. We are already acquainted. We have been attending the same church for years.'

'The Scouts starts at 6.00 pm. Can you get to the drill hall by 5.30 pm?'

'Yes Sir!' said Reggie.

Reggie couldn't wait for Tuesday. Monday dragged by. He walked to the village shop with Lindy who became a little bored with all the talk about what Reggie would do once he became a scout.

'You'll have to smarten yourself up!' said Lindy. 'I don't know if they will let you join, looking like that!'

'What are you talking about?' said Reggie indignantly. 'I'm wearing my best braces.'

Lindy sighed. 'Well, where do I start?'

'My shirt is clean; Auntie Bee gave me a clean shirt this morning.'

'Well!' said Lindy and she sighed again. 'You need to do up all the buttons and your tie needs to be put neatly under your collar. AND it needs to be freshly tied every day.'

'That's a waste of time!' said Reggie. 'It's easier if I take it off over my head and put it on the chair ready for the next day. Are you suggesting I untie it every night and retie it every morning?'

'Yes, I am. When you have untied it, you lay it down over the back of your chair and the creases will fall out. AND then it won't look like a ... err ... a rag.'

'You mean you retie your tie every day?'

'Yes, I do! When I am at school.'

'What a waste of time, all that fiddling! It must take you ages.'

'No not at all!' replied Lindy. 'Because I do it every day, I am well practiced. Your shorts could do with an iron too. I'm sure Auntie Bee would do them for you.'

'She does, but I like these shorts. I wear them all the time.'

'So, when Auntie Bee does the ironing, she has to play a silly game of "Hunt Reggie's Shorts"! She hasn't got time chasing after you to get your shorts off to wash and iron them.'

'Oh no, I have two pairs, but they both look like this.'

They reached the shop.

'And your shoes!' said Lindy.

'What's wrong with my shoes?' said Reggie as standing on one leg, he rubbed the toe of shoe up against the socks of the opposite leg.

'Look at them,' said Lindy, 'they are filthy! They are a disgrace!'

Reggie looked down at his feet. His shoes were scuffed and covered in dirt.

'I am sure you can find a shoe cleaning box at Auntie Bee's. If not, we have one, I'm sure Cludgy will let you borrow it.'

'Really?' said Reggie. 'Do you think she might do them for me?'

'REGGIE!' Lindy yelled. 'No, she won't and you are not to ask her. You are so lazy.'

Once in the shop their attention was now on the jobs Cludgy had asked them to do. They bartered Cludgy's eggs for some tins of fruit which had managed to be imported despite the troubles in the Atlantic with U-boats. They bought a loaf of bread, some flour and some biscuits.

They each took a heavy shopping bag and wandered back along the lane.

'I've been here for over a year now,' said Lindy.

'Yes, that right, and I've been here longer ... since September 1939.'

'Feels like forever,' said Lindy.

'Yeah forever!' said Reggie.

They finished the journey back to the cottages in silence, just enjoying each other's company. Reggie wasn't racing ahead and chatting about his next adventure. Lindy wasn't hurrying, trying to keep up with her friend. They were contented with life and contented enough just to stroll home.

5
Tuesday

Auntie Bee had done her best to smarten up the usual dishevelled appearance of Reggie. She felt that a neat appearance would in some way draw attention away from his naughty cheeky behaviour.

She had ironed his shirt and shorts. All buttons were fastened on his shirt and his tie was straight. They found some garters to hold up his socks and his shoes were polished. She wanted him to make the right impression as he entered the Drill Hall.

Reggie was persuaded not to ride his bike to the hall. Auntie Bee wanted to be with him when they arrived, and keeping up with Reggie on his bike was impossible. She considered the unsuitability of the large size of Reggie and small size of his bike. Despite both being on foot, Auntie Bee had to call out many times, 'Slow down Reggie! I can't keep up.' Reggie was excited to get there.

They walked down the steep gravel hill from the main road. There was a house on their right which had many levels of garden. 'Look at the vegetables growing over there,' said Reggie. 'They are all over the place.'

'Before the war their garden was something to behold,' said Auntie Bee. 'I remember going to a fund-raising garden party there, and the flower beds were just beautiful. Their garden was the envy of everyone in the village.'

Reggie inspected the scene. *Looks pretty good now, with all those vegetables growing, I bet they are still envied.* He thought.

At the side of the house Auntie Bee spotted some firemen. They were cleaning their water pump. 'Firemen! Look Auntie Bee!' shouted Reggie. 'In that posh house and garden!'

'Yes, I know William told me there was a sub-station here.'

'I wonder if they were the ones that came to Little Bridge church the day my dad removed an incendiary and put out a fire in the gallery.'

Mr Knott was at the door waiting for them. 'Hello!' he called. 'Come on in!'

The hall was like a very large shed. The walls were made of wooden planks, and in them there were windows down each side. There was a stage at the end facing the entrance. Their feet clattered on the wooden floor as Reggie and Auntie Bee followed Mr Knott down the hall towards the stage.

Gosh, they've got curtains as well as blackouts here, thought Reggie.

Those curtains need a good clean, thought Auntie Bee.

There was a table next to the stage in the middle, on which were some papers and a pen.

'Do sit down,' said Mr Knott. He moved a chair for Auntie Bee to sit on. Reggie sat down too and scraped the chair on the floor as he moved it towards the table.

Auntie Bee cringed. *Will he ever learn a bit of decorum?* She thought. *Perhaps not, he's Reggie!*

'Now ... the Scout Movement.' said Mr Knott. 'Do you know anything about being a Scout Reggie?'

'No, not really Sir,' said Reggie. 'They wear nice uniforms though. We met two boys pushing a cart up the hill when they were collecting salvage.'

'That was Peter and Bill,' said Mr Knott.

'We, that is Arthur and me,' said Reggie, 'helped them push the heavy load up the hill.'

'Good, helping others is a good principle of any scout.'

'Anyway, they told me that you have fun here.' he paused. 'You play games and football and ...' Reggie hesitated. *That was not the right thing to say, he thought,* so he added, 'and you do a lot of helping other people.'

'That's right we do,' said Mr Knott. 'By the way the boys call me Skipper. Would you like to call me Skipper?'

Reggie felt important. 'Yes please, sir, I mean Skipper sir.'

'Now let me tell you all about the scouts. It was on 24th January way back in 1908, the Boy Scouts movement began in England. It all started with a book written by a man called Baden-Powell entitled 'Scouting for Boys'. It was widely read throughout the country, and consequently lots of impromptu troops of boys started all over Britain.'

'Do I have to read this book?' asked Reggie.

'No lad you don't. I do have a copy but it is very important to me, so I don't lend it to others. Baden-Powell or BP as he is referred to, signed my copy,' he said proudly.

That's a relief! thought Reggie. *I'd never get through a whole book.*

Mr Knott then went on to tell Reggie about a camping expedition for a group of boys to Brownsea Island in Dorset, where the boys learnt how to camp, observe, do woodcraft, and most important of all he taught them patriotism and chivalry.

Reggie didn't understand the word chivalry, but thought it best not to ask at this time.

Mr Knott cleared his throat, and continued. 'Here at the 1st Little Bridge Scout Troop, you will be taught a lot of skills, and you can gain badges. These are to be sewn on to your scout uniform shirt.

Auntie Bee chuckled. *I bet I know who will sew those on!* she thought.

Mr Knott must have read her thoughts as he said, 'The idea is that the boys learn the skill of sewing and do it themselves.'

She couldn't resist a broad grin. Reggie hoped that she would forget what he had said and do the job.

'What are the badges for?' Reggie asked.

'For all sorts of skills. What do you like doing in your spare time?'

'Football,' he said, 'I'm very good at that. And drawing and painting; I'm good at that too.'

'Yes, he is good at his art,' enthused Auntie Bee.

'Oh err … and I have worked with Arthur on the allotments and in the garden … and there are vegetables grown in a small patch at school … but I'm leaving there so I won't be able to garden on that patch.'

'There are badges for gardening and art. You may like to work towards those first. But for the time being we are working on skills that will help the war effort. Today we are going to focus on the First Aid badge and learn how to put on a sling.'

'For someone with a broken arm?' Reggie suggested.

'That's right, but we will have time for some games too. Now the uniform. These are a little difficult to find, but we have a box of spare shirts and ties to get you started.'

'Like Lindy! Her new school uniform came out of the second-hand box too.'

Mr Knott went into the small room at the side of the stage and returned with a cardboard box. He opened it to reveal lots of Scout uniform shirts, they had been added to the box in a haphazard way. Auntie Bee leaned over the box and started to take out items, and held them up against Reggie.

Some boys started to arrive and the room was full of chatter.

'Evening Skipper,' said the boys in turn as they came through the door.

Malcolm from school waved at the group seated in front of the stage. 'Hello Reggie, have you come to join us?' he called. Two boys got out a flag pole.

'That's for the Union Jack!' said Mr Knott. 'It is flown at every session. It is Eagle patrol's responsibility to get it ready this week.'

Mr Knott stood up. 'Take a ball,' he called, 'and go and play football outside on the green, it is a fine evening. I am busy sorting out some uniform for Reggie with Mrs Brown. Reggie, why don't you go and join them?'

Mr Knott did not have to raise his voice much to be heard. As soon as he stood up the boys were quiet and his deep brown voice filled the hall.

On the way-out Reggie spotted lots of bikes leaning up against the fence. They were of all sizes. *I could have brought my bike,* he thought.

Auntie Bee had emptied the box full of shirts. 'I'm afraid these are all too small,' she said.

'Not to worry, I've more upstairs,' he said.

Upstairs, I thought this was a shed! thought Auntie Bee.

He led her through the tiny kitchen to the small flight of stairs at the back.

It was the entrance to the stage and the floor was covered in boxes. 'We keep our camping equipment here as well as show costumes and more spare uniforms.'

'The stage is not much used for performances at the moment then?' asked Auntie Bee.

'Not at the moment, but it can be cleared out if needs be. It's the bell tents that take up the most room. We also have paperwork concerning the troop.' He handed Auntie Bee a small booklet which contained details of the badges the scouts can do once they are enrolled.

'Oh yes,' said Mr. Knott, 'here is a booklet about the scouts and it also includes the promise they make.'

'Thank you!' said Auntie Bee

'And oh … can you take great care of it, as I can't get any more owing to the war and the restrictions in printing and paper.'

'Of course, I understand.'

Auntie Bee was left on her own to continue to go through the boxes of uniform shirts, shorts and even some socks, until she was satisfied that she had found a complete uniform that would fit Reggie and was in good condition. Auntie Bee came out of the kitchen carrying a shirt and a pair of shorts over her arm.

'Did you find everything you need?' said Mr Knott

'Oh yes thank you. I didn't find a scarf and one of those leather ring type things that you fasten the tie with.'

'I will present him with his scarf when he makes his promise, and he will make a woggle that will fix the tie. It will be made of plaited leather. We'll show him how to do that.'

'What about the hat?' said Auntie Bee, I think he finds that most becoming. If that is the right word to be used.'

'Leave that one with me, I'll try and find one in time for his enrolment. I must return to the troop and start the meeting. Have you any more questions for me before I go?'

'No, I don't think so ...' Auntie Bee looked around. 'Just the one then. Where on earth do you put all this stuff when you need to clear the stage?'

Mr Knott laughed. 'There's nothing of great value here, so we put up a couple of tents, and the boys pack them away in there, we make sure it is all off the ground of course, we want to keep the boxes completely dry.'

'Forgive me but I must get back to the boys, it's time to start now.'

Mr Knott escorted Auntie Bee to the door, said goodbye and went around the corner to where the boys were playing football.

As Auntie Bee retraced her steps along the main road, she pondered about how much sewing she had to do to bring this rather dilapidated uniform she had found. Mending the pockets on the front should be a straight forward job, but there was a hole where a badge had been removed, obviously to add to another shirt. The shirt was made of a rather course linen. The shorts just needed the seam to be repaired. I'll wash both of them first, then press them. The shirt was going to be difficult to iron. I'll have to use a wet cloth to steam out the creases.

The more she thought about the job of doing the repairs the more the hole got bigger in her mind, and the seam got longer.

I've got some flour to spare and I could add some margarine and ask Cludgy to do the sewing in return for the flour and margarine. A swap. 'I'll ask Cludgy she'll help me.' she said to herself.

6
Badges

Throughout the spring of 1941 the Germans kept up their bombing campaign of cities and towns on the mainland. To get to their destination they flew over the Island. Consequently, the island residents were on constant alert. Ryde recorded its 500th air raid during this time. In one month, there had been 109.

Once the air raid warning was sounded, the children obediently, despite often being half asleep, struggled out of their beds and went to their Anderson shelters. There was no rush and no panic. Lindy and Reggie climbed into their bunk beds and despite the noise of the planes flying over and went back to sleep. The next day no-one spoke about it as it was becoming routine. They spoke about other things. Reggie's main topic of conversation was his forthcoming enrolment into the scouts. If the raid was during the day and they were deep in a game, this was immediately abandoned as they went to a shelter.

Reverend Peterson opened the vestry door to the church yard one day, when he heard a rather pompous voice saying,

'On my honour I promise that I will do my best,' there was a pause. The rector stood still, and then with an increased vigour the voice continued, 'To do my duty to God.' And yet again here was another pause. Then in a different tone altogether the voice continued, 'and the king.' Then with an increased dramatic tone, 'to help!' then the voice was silent and then he shouted, 'other people, ... at all times ... and to obey the scout law.'

There was silence and then the same voice in a quieter tone said, 'Well done Reggie, you know that really well now.'

'Yes, well done Reggie,' said Reverend Peterson. 'You do know your promise very well.'

'Oh, hello Reverend,' said Reggie without a trace of embarrassment of being caught talking to himself. 'I do want to get it right.'

Reggie, clutching his scout pamphlet, hopped up on to the flat tomb stone under the Yew tree;

'May I join you?' said the vicar.

'Yes of course,' said Reggie as he shuffled up to make more room. With equal dexterity the vicar hopped up on to the gravestone.

'You like sitting here, don't you?' said Reverend Peterson.

'Yes, I sat here with my dad when I met up with him in the middle of the night. We sat here and talked.' He paused and looked at the ground. 'Of course, I don't know where my dad is at the moment, so I sit here and think of him.'

'Good idea.'

'I'm not doing anything wrong sitting on the tombstone, I mean … **he …**,' and Reggie paused and pointed down, 'the person who is buried here, won't mind will he.'

'Good heavens no of course not. It's a good place for you to sit and think of your dad.'

'That's alright then. I don't know if he is safe. I know he was in France when he went missing. He kept my letters in a tobacco tin, and that was French.'

'I heard that too. There are a lot of things that we must not know about. All will be revealed when this war is over.'

'It will end won't it, vicar?' said Reggie.

'Oh yes, it will end one day. Are you still writing to your dad?'

'Yes, I send him pictures too. I'll write and tell him about us sitting here having a chat.'

'Are you going to draw a picture of me?'

'Yes! I won't make you ugly, I promise!'

Reverend Peterson laughed. 'I hadn't thought of that! Will you show it to me before you send it, I would love to see it. May I make one suggestion about your promise?' said Reverend Peterson, 'and that is, you deliver those words in a more normal Reggie type voice. Your delivery was a little over dramatic.'

'Oh yes of course I will, I may be daft but not that daft. It's just that practising it in different voices makes it more interesting. I won't do that on the day!'

'When is your enrolment?'

'This Tuesday!'

'Are you nervous?'

'No, I don't think so!' said Reggie. 'I want to get on with the badges.'

'Which ones are you going to work towards?'

'We are already doing first aid in the hall at present; we have been working on that since my first week.'

'Very important one,' said the vicar.

'But I like the idea of Gardening, Dispatch Rider and Fireman.'

'My goodness, that's a lot of work.'

'Yes, I know but they are important for war work, and I want to "do my bit" as they say.'

'That is very noble of you, but what about yourself. There is an Artist badge,' suggested Reverend Peterson. 'I know you like creating pictures.'

'Yes, I know I have looked at that one, but that is just fun. I thought I had better to do the serious ones first.'

'Let yourself have some enjoyment, Reggie. People love your pictures.'

'I suppose so! There is an awful lot to do in the badge other than just painting a picture you know.'

'I'm quite sure there is. Let's have a look at it.'

Reggie pulled the small booklet out of his pocket and found the artist badge.

'Doing the art work is simple. I draw and paint all the time. I've not tried out modelling in clay yet. 'I haven't got any and wouldn't know where to buy it. That's if I had any money to buy anything!'

'Stop putting barriers in the way,' said Reverend Peterson. 'You just don't know what may turn up.'

'I could of course try sculpting. Arthur gave Cludgy a fish which he had carved out of a piece of drift wood. Then it says I have to find out about an artist who does the modelling or sculpting. There is so much to find out.'

'Reggie, you are not expected to discover everything by yourself. There are always people you can ask. For example, did you know we had two artists who are connected to our church.'

'Really?' said Reggie.

'Do you know Miss Drawbridge who lives in Quarry Lane?'

'Yes, does she live in the bungalow near the field with the horse who is called Black Shadow in it?'

'That's the one, her brother Charles Vaughan Drawbridge who died last year was a sculptor. He assisted Sir Adrian Jones who created the Quadriga in London.'

'The what?' said Reggie.

'It's a big statue in London at Hyde Park Corner. Miss Drawbridge can show you photos taken during its construction. There is one where Sir Adrian and Charles Vaughan Drawbridge are sitting in the shell of one of the horses drinking tea!'

'Why?'

'To get themselves in the papers probably,' said Reverend Peterson. 'And then there is Miss Gwendoline Doubray who is a water colour artist. We have some artistic talent in Little Bridge ... apart from Reggie Mitchell.'

Reggie looked at him as he didn't quite understand what he meant. When he did, he laughed.

'I'm not that good,' he said.

'Ah but you will be.'

'I've some books in my loft about famous artists, when you have decided which form of art you are going to do, I'll look out the right book for you to read through.'

'Thanks so much,' said Reggie. 'You are really kind. I didn't know you were artistic too.'

'I'm not, but I do like looking at beautiful pictures and sculptures.'

The noise of barking preceded the arrival of Texi.

'It's your lunch time Reggie,' called Lindy.

They got down from the tomb stone. Reggie found a stick, he threw it, and Texi chased after him.

'Reverend Peterson?'

'Yes Reggie,'

'You tell us to love everyone. That's easy to love everyone in the village; most people are easy to love. But loving everyone; does that include Hitler?'

'Now that is a tricky one indeed!' said Reverend Peters. 'Leave that one with me.' Using Texi and his stick as a distraction from the question, he escaped.

7
Smiles

The sun beat down on Reggie's back as he worked on gaining his gardener's badge in Arthur's allotment. As soon as he possibly could, Reggie had started on his gardener's badge.

'It takes a long time to do this one as the process of growing plants takes time. So, start now! Reggie.' said Skipper. 'By the way, any work you do for Mr Sparrow on his allotment can go towards your National Service Award.'

Another badge! thought Reggie. *I'll soon have a shirt full.'*

'You must record the number of hours you do, and this needs to be verified by Mr Sparrow.'

Reggie looked confused. 'Verified, what does that mean?'

'Mr Sparrow must sign to confirm the amount of time you do. I'll look you out a form when we next meet at the Scout Hut.'

'You are being so helpful Reggie,' said Arthur. Thinking to himself that he liked this idea of Reggie working on a badge whilst doing hard work on his allotment.

Reggie thrust his fork into the soil and leant it backwards and lots of potatoes appeared at the surface. 'Magic!' he said to himself. 'Just magic!'

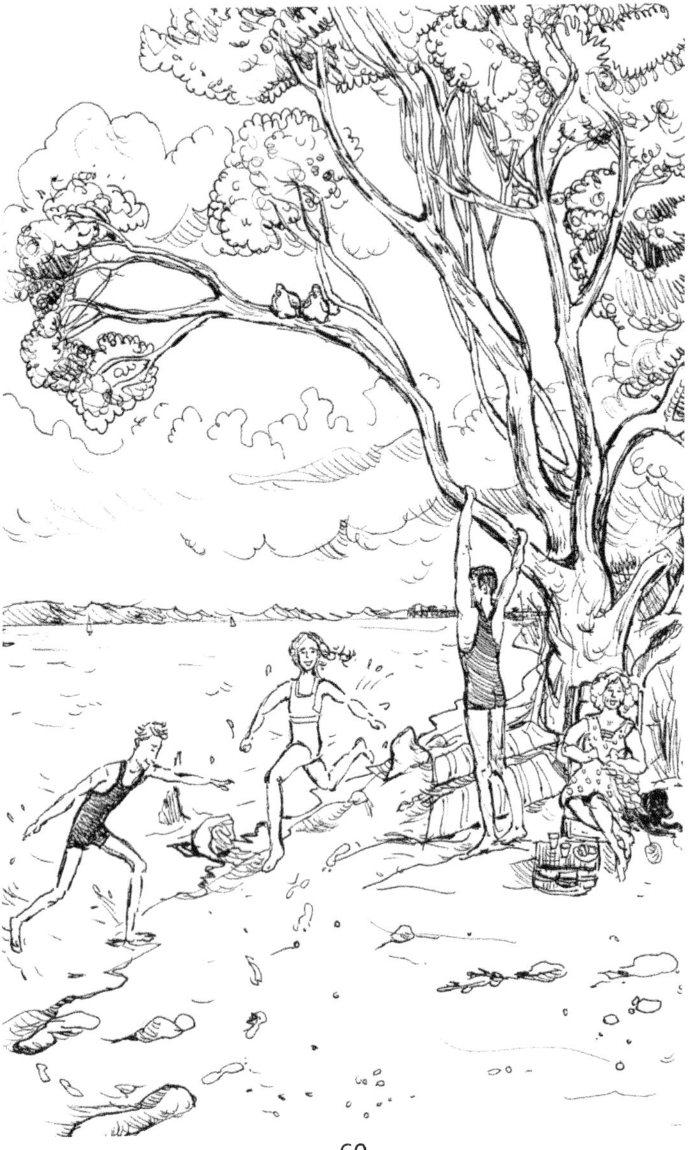

Arthur spotted the pile of potatoes that appeared. 'That's a good haul. Thank you very much,' he called out. Reggie did not hear he was too busy, digging up more potatoes.

Lindy was busy too but her job was less strenuous as she was picking raspberries. Arthur was harvesting a large crop of tomatoes.

Cludgy joined them carrying a tray on which were four glasses of water. Texi had preceded her bounding into the field. He raced around, ending up at each gardener expecting a greeting, which he received in turn. He was quite happy then to chase after the birds who were settling on some of the raspberries.

'He'd make a good scarecrow!' said Cludgy.

Arthur drank his full glass of water without stopping. 'Ahh! Just what is needed,' said Arthur.

Reggie tried to copy the feat, but failed as he gulped down the liquid.

Lindy was more gracious, but even so she drank hers speedily.

'My, my, you were all thirsty,' said Cludgy.

The workers stretched out and laid back on the sweet-smelling grass.

'The sky is a true blue; the crops are ripening. Isn't this all so lovely?' said Reggie.

Arthur and Lindy lifted their heads from the grass and looked at Reggie. Cludgy too turned towards him.

'Ah yes,' said Arthur, 'not satisfied with painting beautiful pictures, Reggie Mitchell is turning towards poetry and prose.'

'What's prose?' asked Reggie.

'Poetry that doesn't rhyme ... I think,' said Lindy.

Cludgy turned to the group and announced, 'How about having lunch on the beach today?' Texi who was enjoying Reggie's company, had rested his head on his lap. He heard the word 'beach' and sprung up and barked his approval at the idea.

'Oh yes,' said Lindy and Reggie. 'Can we go swimming too?'

'If the tide is in of course!'

'I've made sandwiches for lunch; I'll pack them into the basket we use for air raids.'

'What about a flask of tea?' asked Arthur.

'Yes, and a bottle of squash for Lindy and Reggie.' The garden tools were gathered up quickly and carried back to the shed in the walled garden.

An extra sandwich was made for Reggie, and the remains of yesterday's cake was cut evenly into four, packed in a tin and added to the basket.

Reggie rushed home to put on his swimming costume. He grabbed the first towel he could find which he put around his shoulders. He didn't put his shirt on or change his heavy shoes he had worn for gardening.

'What about your shirt?' called Auntie Bee. 'And aren't you going to change your weighty shoes?'

'No time for that!' shouted Reggie as he rushed out of the door. 'Lindy! Lindy! Hurry up!'

Lindy was a little more conscious of her appearance. Over her swimming costume she slipped on her sun dress, put on her sandals, and collected her towel which she rolled into a sausage, and put under her arm.

Arthur picked up the rather old and battered deck chair. The head rest had broken off. Arthur had mended this with a piece of wood, but it was waiting for a cushion to be attached to it. But upholstery was not one of Cludgy's skills, and the job was still waiting to be finished.

Cludgy, the picnic basket in one hand took Arthur's arm and together walked through the grounds of the Quays towards the beach. Lindy, and Reggie with Texi at his heels were much further ahead, could be heard shouting, but not to be seen.

'Is the tide in?' said Lindy who was a little behind Reggie.

'Can't see it yet.'

Reggie took every short cut he could find, but in his gardening boots he was able to negotiate the brambles and rough ground at great speed. His bare legs however, took a bit of a battering.

'It's in! It's in!' he shouted. **'IT'S IN!'** Texi barked loudly just in case no-one heard the exiting news as to the situation of the tide.

'Don't go in the water until I get there,' said Arthur who was a long way back.

Reggie was the first to arrive at the beach, he found a space in front of his favourite tree which was easy to climb. He threw down his towel, sat down and undid his heavy shoes. Lindy was just behind and laid her towel neatly on the sand, sat on it and she too removed her shoes and then pulled off her dress.

Now ready for their bathe, they heard Arthur's warning again. 'Don't go in the water until I'm there.'

They walked forward as close to the sea as they could get without getting their feet wet, thus obeying the instruction of not going in the water until Arthur was there. They danced forward and backwards avoiding getting their feet wet as the waves lapped in. Texi did not like deep water, he splashed around the children's legs.

'Alright you two, in you go,' called Arthur. 'I'm here now.'

The children charged forward and fell into the lovely cool clear water.

'What's it like?' shouted Arthur.

'Lovely!' said Lindy. Texi did not agree, he returned to sit by Cludgy where he felt safe.

'You stay with me Texi,' said Cludgy. 'Good boy, settle down.'

'Are you coming in?' asked Reggie.

Arthur took off his shoes, his shirt and trousers, to reveal a full-length swimming costume.

'Here I come!' yelled Arthur. What a sight greeted the children as he ran down the beach into the sea, yelling as he went. They were seeing an Arthur Sparrow they had never seen before. Once in the water he dived under and came up close to the children and pretended to be a monster, making monster type arm movement, and monster type noises.

Lindy and Reggie ran and then swam away. Shrieking, laughing and screaming as they went.

On the beach seated on the battered chair Cludgy smiled as she watched the lovely scene developing in front of her.

Oh this beastly war. How much more I could enjoy this if there wasn't the constant worry of the war raging away. Cludgy slipped a lead on Texi's collar and secured it to the tree. She had chosen a shady spot and Texi soon settled down. Next she busied herself setting the plates and cups on a table cloth on the sand. After warning the children to swim parallel to the shore, Arthur swam out towards the mainland. Cludgy hated him doing that, but was assured that he was a good swimmer.

Lindy swam a strong breaststroke, Reggie did the arm movements but had never been taught the stroke, so his legs made a mixture of splash and circles. This was one occasion where Lindy was much faster than Reggie and had to wait for him.

After a while Arthur got out and walked up the beach. 'Call the children in,' said Cludgy. 'Let's have some lunch.'

Lindy and Reggie swam into the shore and raced up the beach.

'First one to get to Cludgy,' said Arthur, 'is the winner!'

'Mind the food!' shouted Cludgy. 'You won't want your sandwiches covered in sea water and sand.'

She turned to her husband. 'Arthur Sparrow just how old do you think you are?'

Arthur smiled and shrugged his shoulders.

The children's towels were ready to be sat on for lunch. 'How are we to get dry?' asked Lindy.

'The sun is shining; we could pretend to be washing on the washing line.' With his arms outstretched Reggie revived his RAF aeroplane dance. 'I'm a Spitfire! I'm a Spitfire!' he yelled as he made Spitfire engine noises, whilst running around the beach. Much to the children's joy, three aeroplanes flew overhead.

'Spitfires! spitfires!' shouted Reggie.

Lindy joined in, the two children ran around, firing their imaginary machine guns.

They sat down on their towels ready for lunch. 'Clean hands?' asked Cludgy.

The children brushed the sand from their hands, then six hands appeared outstretched in front of Cludgy. She sniggered and then said, 'Palms up!' she scrutinised all six. 'Pass! Hands Down!' They turned them over. 'Alright, pass. Although I am not sure about Arthurs right little finger!' Arthur licked it and presented it again! Cludgy looked at her husband and giggled.

'Let's eat!' said Cludgy.

The sun continued to beat down. The sky was a vivid blue as was the sea, there was a gentle cooling breeze and the waves made a gentle lapping sound.

'Do you know? said Cludgy, 'except for the war, it couldn't have been a more glorious day.'

After they had eaten their lunch, the children wanted to go back into the sea. 'You must wait an hour; you can get cramp if you swim too soon after eating.'

'Can we sit in the surf on the shore line?'

'Good idea!' said Arthur. He watched the children go down to the surf, then he made a pillow by rolling up Lindy's towel. He put it behind his head, held it there as he stretched his body and lay back on the sand.

Cludgy had just picked up her knitting. 'Oh!' she said. 'Going to have a nap, are you? I'll watch the children in the water then?'

'If you would please?'

'Good thing I have three eyes. One for my knitting and the other two for the children. The pattern is so easy, I don't need to look at my work much if at all.'

8
A Scout Whistles

For a while Lindy and Reggie sat contentedly on the shore line and watched the waves gently roll in and draw away. Each wave covered their feet and then sucked away taking some sand with it. The sound was very gentle and soothing.

They were deep in their own thoughts. Lindy thought of the day trips she had taken with her mother and father. They never came to Little Bridge beach; when they came to the island before the war, they went to Ryde. But she was sure that she would have liked it. Their day trips included sandcastles, playing in the sunshine and having an ice cream.

Reggie too thought of his dad and mum. He had told them about joining the scouts. He had had to write two separate letters. Although his writing had improved, completing two letters was quite an achievement. He so wanted his dad to be proud of him. Suddenly Reggie said out loud, 'I want to be useful!'

Lindy turned to him. 'What did you say?'

'You see Lindy, my dad is in the army fighting for king and country, my mum is building bits for Spitfires and here I am wanting to do my bit too.'

'Reggie we are not old enough to worry about that. We have to go to school so we can eventually get a job. This war will end one day.'

'I know that's what Reverend Peterson said,' continued Reggie.

'Why are you worried about this now?'

'I'm going to become a scout! I get enrolled on Tuesday.'

'I know,' said Lindy, 'I've heard you practicing your promise.'

'Ah but that is just the start, I am going to do badges, and learn lots of things that could be useful.'

'I know you are working on your Gardeners badge; you were toiling on the allotment this morning.'

'But I want to do my Fireman's badge too, so I can put out fires, my First Aid badge to help with the wounded if needs be and then there's the Dispatch Rider, so I can deliver important messages wherever they are needed.'

'That's a lot of work to do, isn't it?' said Lindy. 'I don't expect that you are meant to do it all at once.'

Reggie wasn't listening. 'Then' he continued, 'I really want to do the Artists Badge.'

'Oh, you will sail through that, you are always drawing and painting.'

'I know, but there are other forms of art. I'd like to try carving and modelling in clay for example.

Then I have to discover famous artists who painted, carved or modelled and look at their work. You see painting a picture is the easy bit.'

'Oh Reggie, why do you always want things now, this minute. There's plenty of time.'

Reggie was silent. Deep in his thoughts again. 'Then there is one more thing I have got to be able to do.'

'Oh, what's that?'

'It's nothing really.' Reggie paused and turned his head away and dug his fingers into the sand and moved it forwards and backwards.

'What is it then?' said Lindy. 'It must be something, it can't be nothing.' Lindy knew her friend too well.

'Well Lindy don't laugh, will you?'

'No of course not,' Lindy assured him.

'Well, I'll tell you then. Promise you won't laugh?'

'I won't laugh! I promise, I won't laugh.'

'Well, I'll tell you then.' There was another pause.

'Well then tell me!' Lindy was getting a little exasperated.

'I can't whistle,' he muttered.

'You can't do what?' asked Lindy.

He leant towards Lindy and whispered in her ear. 'Whistle. I can't whistle.'

'Why do you need to whistle?'

'Because number eight in this little booklet I was given, says that 'a scout whistles and is cheerful under all difficulties.' And I can't whistle, I have tried and tried, but I can't whistle.'

Lindy smiled, but stifled a laugh. She quickly changed the shape of her mouth to a more serious position. 'Oh Reggie, is that all?'

'But everyone else can do it, and there I will be with all the boys but not able to whistle. Oh, Lindy what shall I do? They are going to think that I'm stupid!'

'Reggie Mitchell!' said Lindy crossly. 'You are not stupid! Not at all! I'll teach you to whistle.'

'See! Even you can whistle and I can't.'

'Look, you make your lips like this and ...'

'I know how to shape my mouth, but every time I blow, spit comes out and no whistle.'

'Then don't blow so hard!'

Reggie tried and failed.

'It'll take time, said Lindy. 'I'll ask Arthur if he knows how to whistle and then he can teach you.'

'No don't! I don't want everyone to know.'

'It's only Arthur, if I tell him not to tell anyone else, he won't. You can trust Arthur.'

The tide had come in higher and Lindy and Reggie were now sitting in water over their legs and up to their waists. A large log which was just below the high-tide mark had floated into the water and in front of the children.

They jumped up walked into the sea to retrieve it. 'Woops! We forgot to ask Arthur,' said Lindy.

'Can we get back into the water?' Lindy called.

'Please!' said Reggie.

Cludgy put her knitting aside and nudged Arthur. 'Wake up! They want to get back into the water.'

After a yawn and a few grunts from Arthur who had been roused from a very deep sleep he said, 'What! … Yes … in the water again. Off you go. What have they found?'

'It's a log I think,' said Cludgy

Lindy swam out to collect it. She put her hands on the end and pushed it along to shallow water using her breaststroke kick.

The log was about two yards long, the ends were sawn and flat and it was quite thick. It had been in the sea for a long while as it was quite smooth except for a few spikey bits where small branches had stuck out. They rolled on to the log and tried to push it along, just kicking their legs. They fell off. This time they faced each other and rolled on again. They turned in a circle but had a little more success as they stayed on longer. However, Reggie got too ambitious and pushed his body on further, thus upsetting the balance and so they fell off again.

'Lindy, will you hold it whilst I try and ride it like a horse?'

Lindy obliged and whilst she held it tight, Reggie managed to get on. But once she let go his balance failed, the log rolled over and he fell off.

Hearing the splashing and squealing coming from the sea, Cludgy stopped knitting and looked up.

'Just look at those two, what fun they are having,' said Cludgy. 'Arthur, just look at them!'

The two of them sat still for a while watching the spectacle laughing at the children's antics. 'They are like a couple of clowns at a circus,' said Arthur.

Cludgy finished her knitting and cast off. 'That's the back finished, only the sides to go,' she said.

'What's that dear?' said Arthur.

'I've finished the back, I have just the sides to do!'

Arthur burst out laughing again as Reggie repeatedly fell off.

'Look! he's fallen off again!' he said. 'Just look at those children.' The children's excitement roused Texi who got up to investigate. Cludgy untied his lead and the dog bounded down towards the waters edge. She knew full well that he would go no further as he did not like deep water, so he sat and watched the antics, waiting for them to finish, come out of the sea and play with him again.

'Aren't they having a lovely time,' said Cludgy. 'This is a truly memorable day.'

She packed her knitting away in the basket and collected up the picnic plates and cups. 'I'm ready for a fresh cup of tea, let's call the children in and get home. The tide is going out and I think the weather is changing.'

Arthur yawned. 'What a perfect afternoon!' he announced.

'How do you know; you have been asleep for the most part of it. Go and call the children in. My teapot is beckoning me to come home.'

Arthur was envious of the enjoyment the children were having playing with the log in the sea. He watched quietly for a while but then he could contain his composure no longer and ran down the beach, charged into the water, dived under the waves and surfaced just in front of the log. Texi perked up, expecting Arthur to join him on the beach, when he didn't the dejected dog returned to his sitting position to watch.

Once in the water Arthur joined in. It was to take quite a while for Cludgy to persuade the three of them to get out of the water. They were having far too much fun. With Arthur holding the log, Lindy and Reggie could straddle it. They were facing Arthur so when he pushed them along, they were travelling backwards. He tipped it up so they would fall in.

'Sorry,' he mocked, 'that was done quite by accident.'

'Fibber!' Reggie shouted.

'Let's face the other way, said Lindy. Arthur held on, and they climbed on the log again. 'Hold tight! I have a very fast engine on this motorised log.'

He pushed the log along, Lindy held tight to Reggie as they progressed as fast as Arthur could go. To add to the effect, he made engine noises.

It was Cludgy who stopped the play, the light was fading, she needed to get supper, and Arthur was on duty later that evening.

'Come on in you three children! Yes, Arthur that means you too.'

They pushed the log high up on the beach away from the high-water mark. They wanted to ride the motorised log again another day.

Lindy looked for her towel. 'Where's my towel please.'

'It's hanging on the tree. Arthur and Reggie, yours are there too.'

'Thanks,' said Lindy as she went to the tree to pull her towel off the branch. 'Gosh it is all sandy.'

'What do you expect?' said Cludgy.

'Hadn't you noticed,' said Reggie, 'the beach is full of it.'

'I shook the towels out as hard as I could,' said Cludgy. 'But they are a little damp so the sand sticks.'

Reggie dropped his, adding more sand to his rather small towel. Then he repeated his RAF dance holding the towel in the air with both hands. 'This is my parachute!' he shouted. Texi joined in, he obviously thought that this activity was for him. They had made a game for Texi! He raced around the children's legs barking.

Cludgy smiled at the happy scene. 'It has been a lovely day. Hasn't it Arthur?'

'Yes, it has my love, just look how happy they are.'

'Everything would be just perfect except for this beastly war.'

Cludgy picked up the basket, and started to walk back. Arthur picked up the deck chair and quickened his step to catch his wife up. He took her hand.

'Come on Texi, here boy!' Arthur called. The dog now with replenished energy, raced up the path towards the cottages and home.

Lindy slipped her dress on over her wet costume and put her shoes on over her sandy feet. Reggie only had his pair of gardening boots to put on, so with his towel around his shoulders he walked with Lindy back to the cottages.

'How on earth am I supposed to whistle,' said Reggie, 'if I to look cheerful at the same time.'

9
Lindy's First Day

Lindy felt very smart in her school uniform. Cludgy had done a marvellous job renovating the second-hand clothes that Reverend Mother had given her. She washed the shirts, ironed them, and replaced all the buttons so that they matched each other and were in the right place, in line. The gymslip needed the most work, it was too long, and the pleats had been ironed out by constant sitting on wooden school chairs. When she had finished turning up the hem, she pressed the pleats back in again. The tie just needed a good wash as it had remnants of food on it. The hat was creased. *This must have ended up in a pocket or stuffed into a bag to end up looking like this,* Cludgy thought. She stuffed it with paper to make the right shape again and then using the steam from the boiling kettle, she carefully pulled it out so it looked like a beret again.

Her new school shoes were very comfortable and fitted her well. Lindy had polished them the previous night. She carried her school satchel which had faithfully served her at every school she had attended. It had been a present from her mother when she first went to her boarding school in Brighton. At that time, it was enormous for her, but now it was a lot smaller as Lindy had grown.

'The jumpers in the box that Reverend Mother offered me were in an awful state,' Cludgy said. 'I knew that it was virtually impossible to renovate one of those so I didn't take one. I decided to knit a new one myself. I noticed that a lot of the girls have ones that are home knitted.'

She managed to get enough brown wool of the right type to make a new jumper for Lindy.

'Brown is not a popular colour for knitting wool, especially as it has to be quite a fine weave for your school jumper,' said Cludgy. 'That ply is usually for baby clothes.'

Reggie on the other hand, was dressed as usual. His clothes were clean, Auntie Bee had seen to that, but his appearance was as scruffy as usual.

'Reggie' said Lindy at the bus stop.

'What?'

'It's your first day at your new school, don't you want to make a good impression?'

'Why?'

'Because you want to get on! That's why. You want to do well, don't you?'

'How does the way I dress help me to do well at school?'

Lindy sighed. She couldn't answer that. So, she just shook her head from side to side.

'You told me that your dad said that he wanted you to do well and be clever, didn't he?'

'Yes, he did,' said Reggie.

'Well?' said Lindy. 'Is that a good reason why you should make a good impression when you go to school and work hard.'

'Ah but he didn't say anything about how I should dress.'

Lindy gave up and the bus arrived.

They got on the bus and sat on the side seats. Lindy put her bag on her lap. Reggie carried a small lunch box which was tied up with string. Auntie Bee had made a loop out of the spare string making it easier to carry. He didn't have a school bag, as he had not been told to bring one. He did however have a pencil and an exercise book which he had bent in two and squashed in his inside pocket. Lindy on the other hand had been given specific instructions as to what she should bring to school. This included pens and pencils and a rough exercise book. She also carried her lunch box which she had managed to put in her school bag with the flap open.

They got off the bus at John's Street and walked together towards the High Street and then turned right. Parting company at the 'Street of the Stars' as Reggie called it, they went their separate ways to face going to school without each other, their best friend.

Lindy reached the door into the school where she had been before. In front of her was a girl who was in the throes of trying not to cry. 'I don't want to go to school,' she said as she sniffed again.'

'Well, you are going to school, that is what you are meant to do,' said the lady with her. 'So, stop that sniffing and pull yourself together.'

Lindy stood quietly wishing she wasn't there to hear this. She felt as if she were intruding.

'Ring the bell Angela,' said the lady.

Angela refused, pushing her hands further down into her pockets.

'Alright I'll do it,' said the lady, pushing Angela aside she reached for the bell and tugged it.

It was not very long before the door was opened and a nun stood there.

Before anyone could say anything, the nun spoke sharply, 'You are not supposed to come in this entrance, you must go out into the street take the passage on your left and enter through the playground.' She didn't wait for a response, she just shut the door. That was the last straw for Angela, who opened her mouth and wailed!

The lady took a firm hold of Angela's arm and marched her out into the street. She continued to scream at the top of her voice, much to the consternation of other people passing by. Lindy followed the duo down the passage.

When they got to the gate, Lindy felt she couldn't leave this distressed child. 'Shall I take her in for you?' she said to the lady.

She was about to answer when Angela put her arms around the lady's waist and entwined one of her legs around one of the lady's legs.

'No!' she wailed. 'I don't want to go to school!'

This charade continued for quite a while, when the nun who had opened the front door appeared at the gate of the playground.

'Now we can't have this!' she said. 'Stop it at once! ... at once I said.'

Angela stopped. Lindy stood aghast and the lady breathed a sigh of relief.

'Is she your sister?' the nun asked Lindy.

'No thank you,' said Lindy. 'I mean no Sister ... I meant to say no she is not my sister, Sister.'

Angela shied away from the nun and Lindy suddenly felt a warm sticky hand in hers.

'Ah that's good!' said the sister. 'She has found a friend.'

No-one asked me if I want to be her friend, thought Lindy.

'Right now, into the playground you two. The bell will be going soon for you to go to the hall for assembly.'

Angela still had a firm grip on Lindy's hand.

A quiet little voice suddenly mumbled something. Lindy did not understand. She leant towards Angela, 'What did you say?'

'Will you be my friend?' she asked. 'Please.'

'Oh alright, I suppose so. Is this your first day here?'

'Yes, is it yours too?'

'Yes,' said Lindy. 'What class are you in?'

Angela sniffed again. 'Junior four,' she said.

'Oh, I am in Senior one,' said Lindy. 'So, I'm afraid we won't be together. You'll be alright, you'll make friends in your class.'

A bell rang and girls started to move towards the green fire escape staircase. They got to the bottom where a nun stood.

'That's the same one who met us at the gate!' said Angela.

The nun put her hand on Angela's shoulder and said, 'Not you, you go that way to the first classroom around the corner.'

Angela turned to Lindy, 'Oh, please meet me at Lunchtime, oh please, ... I'll have something to look forward to.'

'Oh, alright then ... Lunch time,' said Lindy begrudgingly.

'Get on girls ... do get a move on,' the nun kept continuously shouting.

Lindy walked into the vast hall. The girls were arranged in lines across the room starting with those in Senior One, and finishing with Senior Five. There were some girls from that class who were holding pieces of paper with names on.

'What's your name?' Lindy was asked.

'Lindy Elliot,' she replied.

'Is that your whole name? I can't seem to find it on my sheet.' *Oh that's good maybe I can go home instead.* thought Lindy. She looked at her piece of paper. 'May I help?' she asked.

'Yes, where are you?'

Lindy pointed to her name at the bottom of the long list.

'Oh yes, I've found you. You're a scholarship girl. Go over there. You are in the front row at the end.'

A scholarship girl, thought Lindy, *didn't they all have to pass an exam to get into this school?*

Lindy did not understand the significance of standing at the end of the line, but being labelled a 'scholarship girl' worried her. It had in fact no significance at all.

Reverend Mother appeared at the door; the girls moved aside as she glided into the hall. Her shoes rhythmically thumped on the wooden floor as she seemed to float across the hall to her place at the end in front of the lines of school girls. She gave a welcome speech; a few prayers were said, and then the girls left the hall to go to their classrooms. The prayers that were said had very little meaning for Lindy. They were delivered very fast and Lindy felt were delivered with very little feeling.

The oldest girls left the hall first, then the next and so on until Lindy was the last to leave.

'You look very smart Lindy,' said Reverend Mother Victoire. 'Very smart indeed.'

Lindy wanted to tell her that Cludgy was very clever, but that would take too much time. So, a simple, 'thank you' was given.

'You need to put your coat and hat away in the cloakroom,' said Mother Victoire, 'do you remember where that is?'

'Yes Mother,' said Lindy.

'Go quickly!' The girls in her class had disappeared around the corner. 'Never mind! You know where your classroom is, you can join them as soon as possible.'

It took a while to work out where her peg was, until she found the one that had her name written on a label at the side. She hung her coat and hat up.

When Lindy arrived at the classroom door yet another Hail Mary was being said. She waited until they had finished before entering the room.

'Ah here she is. You are a scholarship entrant, aren't you.'

'Yes sister,' said Lindy. She still had no idea of why passing an exam was such a crime.

'Mother!' said the nun. 'You call me Mother, I am Mother Michael.'

'Oh sorry, … Yes Mother.' Lindy repeated.

'Your desk is over there, near the window.' Lindy went through the line of single desks to her place and sat down.

What a nice place, I can look out of the window. She thought. Lindy remembered how she sat near a window in at her school in Portsmouth, just after her mother had died. She recalled that the teacher Mr Hacker had chastised her when she had finished her work so quickly. She looked out of the convent window onto the playground.

'Pay attention!' shouted Mother Michael. 'Lindy Elliot! you appear to be the only new girl in this class.'

'Am I?' said Lindy a little bemused as to why she was singled out again.

'Our air raid shelter Lindy Elliot, is in the basement of this building, please follow the other girls when the siren is sounded.'

'Yes Mother,' said Lindy. 'I will.'

'I am to be your maths teacher, but now this first half hour is dedicated to Religious Studies. She handed out small books which contained the four gospels and nothing else.

'Now these books are valuable, not only for their content but for the fact that we can't get any more. There is a war on you know.'

Lindy wanted to tell her that she had the four gospels in the bible at home, but thought better of it and decided to remain silent.

They turned to the beginning of St John's gospel and each pupil were told to read a verse in turn. Lindy knew this piece well; she had heard it in church many times. She worked it out that her verse was the last one, number 14, but she was not prepared for what happened next. She started to read, 'And the Word was made flesh, and ...' Mother Michael stood up as did most of the girls in the class; Lindy stopped reading, and then they uniformly knelt down on one knee.

'Carry on girl, carry on!' snapped Mother Michael impatiently. 'Read the rest of the verse.'

Lindy read on, 'And the Word was made flesh, and dwelt among us and we beheld his glory, the glory as of the only begotten of the father, full of grace and truth.'

The nun and the girls got up from their kneeling position and sat down again. Lindy was bemused, she did not know what had happened. Mother Michael did not explain. *How am I to learn, if she doesn't tell me why they knelt down.*

For the next ten minutes she spoke about God being everywhere. *That's right,* thought Lindy, *of course He is. I know that – she doesn't have to go on so.* Then for the next ten minutes she preached that God was not in the non-Catholic church. Lindy's first reaction was horror. *How dare she say that, that is very rude.* Then she saw how ridiculous the statement was. *Did God float around the world saying to Himself 'I'll go there, it is Catholic, but I won't go there it is Church of England!* 'Ridiculous!' Lindy muttered out loud.

'Did someone speak?'

Fortunately, she didn't pursue finding the culprit but simply gave out the homework which was to be learnt by heart. The section was John Chapter 1 verses 1 – 14. Lindy wrote it in her exercise book she had brought with her.

At break time, Lindy who was a scholarship girl, went out to the playground for some respite from the horridness of the class room. The hatefulness continued when one of the girls found out Lindy's father was a fireman.

'My dad's a solicitor. Your Dad is a fifty bob a week army dodger,' she gibed and laughed.

'He worked in that great fire in Portsmouth last January. He put out fires and rescued people. Could your dad have done that working in his office as he does?'

10
Reggie's First Day

Reggie's first day at his new school couldn't have been more different than Lindy's. Although he was a little nervous, Reggie hid this through his bravado. *A Scout whistles and is cheerful under all difficulties!'* He thought to himself. He puckered up his lips and blew, as usual spit came out but there was no whistle. *I must learn how to whistle.* He put an extra spring into his step as he neared the door. Just then from behind him he heard, 'Hey, Reggie, wait for me!' Reggie turned it was Archie from Little Bridge School. He was just as glad to see Reggie as he was to see him.

'Hello,' said Reggie. 'Are you looking forward to this.'

'Yes, I hope we won't have to do all the hard stuffy work we did before.'

'What do you mean?'

'Well,' said Archie, 'you know, Geography, History and such like. I never understood why we have to know where every country is in the world or what they did in the past.'

'Lindy likes all that.' said Reggie

'Yeah, I know!' he said. 'But she is a swot.'

They reached the door to the school, which was open. They were greeted by an older boy with a list in his hand. 'Hello,' he said. 'What are your names?'

'Reggie Mitchell.'

'Archie Carter.'

'I'm David Ford,' said the older boy.

'Hello,' Reggie and Archie said in unison.

David ran his finger down the list. Ah here you are! Reginald and Archibald.'

The boys' faces dropped.

'Only teasing!' said David. 'Reggie, Archie, welcome.'

'Go straight ahead along the corridor to the big hall at the end and wait there. Assembly is in about five minutes.'

It was quiet when they entered the large hall. There was a small stage at one end. The boys looked around.

'It's like church! No-one is speaking!' whispered Reggie.

'Shush,' said Archie.

'Why?' said Reggie.

'Because no-one else is speaking or making a noise.'

Just then the stage was filled with adults. 'They are always silent on the first day,' said the headmaster to his colleague on his left. He moved to the front of the stage. 'Good morning boys,' he said.

'He must be the head master,' whispered Archie.

'Shush!' said Reggie.

'Good morning, sir,' replied the assembled boys.

There was no pretty piano music or hymns as there had been at Little Bridge School. There were a couple of prayers including one for peace and then the head master instructed new boys to remain in the hall and the others go to their classrooms. 'AND quietly!' he said.

'Nothing has changed there!' whispered Reggie. 'Why does walking have to be quiet?'

'Shush!' said Archie.

'Sit down boys!' the headmaster instructed.

'Where?' whispered Archie.

The head master heard. 'On the floor please.' He pulled a blackboard and easel into the centre. 'Gather around boys please. Can you all see the board? Get to a position where you can.'

There was a bit of shuffling towards the board, but eventually they were all still. 'Have you all got a rough book and pencil?'

Reggie pulled out his book from his inside pocket, smoothed it flat and then opened the first page.

'Those who have not, may use some of the scrap paper I have here on the table. … No don't all get up. Put up your hand if you need paper and a piece will be passed to you.' He looked around the room and fixed his eyes on Reggie. 'Err … you boy, what is your name?'

Reggie looked around to check he meant him. 'Who me sir?' he said.

'Yes! What is your name?'

'Reggie Mitchell sir.'

'Reggie, would you pass some paper to those who have none please?'

What importance Reggie felt at that moment.

'Do I give them a pencil if they need one sir?'

'Yes, well done, I failed to mention that.'

He swelled with pride and knew he was going to get on well at this school.

'I want you to copy down your timetable from the board,' the headmaster said.

Reggie was so glad that Lindy had persuaded him that reading and writing was important. He reopened his exercise book, as it had folded by itself as he had left it on the floor when handing out the paper, he wrote as neatly as possible. His lines were straight and his writing was clear. He finished and looked up and saw the head master smile at him. Looking around the room, he realised that he had been the first to finish and there were some who were having trouble.

A hand was raised at the front. 'Please sir I have broken my pencil.'

'Oh dear,' said the head master.

Reggie raised his hand, 'May I help him?' he said.

'Thank you, Reggie, yes please. There is a sharpener by the pencil box on the table.'

Reggie went over, handed the boy his pencil, and then went to the table to sharpened the broken one. When he returned, he noticed the boy was shaking with nerves and having trouble writing. Reggie saw in him what he had been like two years ago when he arrived at Little Bridge. He lent over his page and dictated the timetable word by word and sometimes letter by letter.

Armed with their timetables the class moved, quietly, to Room 3, their classroom for woodwork. They entered the room.

An unseen voice said, 'Boys, go and find yourself a desk as quick as you can.'

The room was furnished with workbenches in two lines. There was a fight for the back two. Reggie chose a place near the front; he felt his new status as the teacher's assistant demanded it. He didn't want to be disturbed by other boys playing around.

Archie took the bench behind him, and the shy boy he had met in the hall was next to him.

Mr Beech introduced himself to the class, took the register and turned to the blackboard on which was written the word; "tools".

'First of all, I want you to go into the drawer in front of you and find an apron and put it on,' Mr Beech said. Whilst you are doing that, I am going to write down the name of a tool and I want you to find one in your desk drawer.'

In the drawer freshly laundered were brown aprons made of thick brown linen. They put them on. For some boys tying a bow behind their backs was difficult. They improvised.

Mr Beech wrote the word "hammer". 'That was easy wasn't it,' he said to the class.

The boys took out hammers and put them on their workbench.

'Now look around the room, there are different types of hammers.' Then he wrote "Claw Hammer and Ball-Pein Hammer".

'Which one have you picked up?'

This game went on for a while, and soon the workbenches were covered in tools.

'We will now have a 15-minute break,' said Mr Beech. 'On your return, I want you to draw each tool in your exercise books adding its name underneath.

The break consisted of a trip to the lavatories, a quick snack if they had one and a chat.

In no time at all they returned to the class room. Reggie was happy. He had done a lot of still life since he had discovered his love of anything to do with art. However, his usual still life had been mostly drawing fruit, bowls, flowers and vases. Drawing a tool was going to be different but easy. He enjoyed quietly drawing each tool so much so that he didn't hear the bell for lunch.

'Aren't you hungry Reggie?' said Mr Beech.

'Yes ... oh excuse me I didn't hear the bell.'

Mr Beech looked at his work. 'You have a talent for drawing Reggie. That is very good.'

Out in the playground, Reggie found Archie and the shy boy he had met that morning.

'This is Terry,' said Archie. 'He lives on a farm near Ashey.'

The three boys sat contentedly chatting whilst eating their lunch until they were asked to join in a game of football. They took off their jumpers and added them to the two piles which made up the goal posts. Reggie was now in his heaven and he quickly showed off his skills at the game. There was a disputed goal scored by Reggie, as he had hit the pile of jumpers, scattering them far and wide.

'That hit the post!' a player said. 'No goal!'

'Definitely no goal,' said another.

'But look where it has landed,' argued Reggie, 'Right in the middle past the goal and in line with the goal posts.'

'No! it definitely would have hit the post and so would have bounced back. Look how it scattered the jumpers,' he replied.

The bell rang for return to lessons becoming the final whistle of the game. The jumpers and jackets that made the goal posts were retrieved and the boys returned to their classrooms.

The afternoon was spent painting a picture. The subject was 'A memorable moment in my life.'

Reggie thought for a while, there were so many moments that he couldn't forget. His dad rescuing him from the hole in the ground was considered, but he thought that too difficult to draw and paint as it was mostly his face, and a lot of black paint as the hole was totally in the dark. He chose to create a picture of the time when he had to lie hiding from the Spitfire which was chasing the

Messerschmidt last summer when he was at the top of Rolling Road. How could he ever forget that moment. It wasn't complicated or difficult as he felt he could add a lot of hills and fields in the picture.

Reggie felt very pleased with himself. His semi smart appearance of that morning had completely disappeared. There was paint on his shirt and shorts, his shoes were scuffed, even his face was dirty. His dishevelled appearance did not detract from his happy smile when he spotted Lindy at the bus stop in John Street.

He had had a lovely time; he had met up with a friend from the village, he had played football with a boy who was in the scouts. His last lesson was art; how could the day have been more pleasant?

11
Learning at the Convent

It could be said that going to high school was a bit of a shock for Lindy. The village school was calm, she never felt hated or uncomfortable. Apart from feeling out of place when she joined the Little Bridge school, there was no hatred. There were jokes played, but nothing horrid.

The high school, run by nuns was so different.

God wasn't portrayed as the loving God that she had been taught about at her church in Little Bridge. He was a super being who punished. The girls sat quietly and learnt about a place called purgatory. 'When you die, you will go to purgatory first before going to Heaven.'

Mother Michael said in an aggressive tone, 'AND depending on how wicked you have been you will have to stay there to atone for your sins.'

Lindy thought of her mother. She had died in January 1940 of cancer. Lindy could not imagine her mother, her loving mother, having to endure any time in this purgatory, her mother was kind hard working and loved everyone.

Lindy decided to ignore this.

'If your homework is not good enough, or someone talks in class, God knows,' Mother Michael continued. 'He knows!'

Again, it was a good thing that there was no homework given out for that lesson as Lindy was angry and ready to write down what she thought.

At Little Bridge School there had been help and support, there had been Miss Simons to whom Lindy could go in times of trouble or difficulty. At this new school there was no-one she felt she could approach. No-one she could go to, to ask questions. She was terrified to ask if she didn't understand something. *If I ask, will the teacher laugh at me because I don't know? The other pupils will probably join in and make fun of me. How am I supposed to learn?*

The other pupils in her class were not much better. She had a friend from a lower class, Angela, but when she travelled with her on the bus she talked so much and so fast that if Lindy wanted to say anything she could not, as Angela never stopped.

The bullying started with name calling. Then the laughter was loud at answers given in class that Lindy got wrong.

'Don't you know that?' snarled Jean, 'Don't you know anything? We do! Your old school must have been pretty awful! Didn't you learn anything there?'

Lindy did not respond; she was embarrassed that she didn't know the answer. *But then if I have never been told or had lesson on the subject how could I give the right reply.* Lindy soon gave up answering questions in class. She didn't notice that when questions were asked no-one else answered. *Perhaps those girls and Jean don't know the answer either.* She realised for herself.

Then one day she couldn't find her coat. The girls had moved it and she missed her bus home searching for it. The situation was not improved as Angela was waiting.

'Haven't you found it yet?' she said as she sat on the shoe lockers banging her heels impatiently against the wooden sides. The coat was eventually found when the room was empty, at the end of the long corridor of coat hooks with the Form V coats.

One of the most horrid ones was to find her hockey boots in her desk on top of her books. She was the last to get to the class room. Jean and her four friends were seated and giggling. She opened her desk to get her books and found her boots. Although they were clean, there was mud and horse droppings spread around all over contents of her desk. As she was cleaning up the mess Lindy suddenly became aware of Bernadette standing at the side of her with a dustpan and brush. Lindy was surprised. She handed it to Lindy.

'Thank you, Bernadette,' she said. The two girls looked at each other and said no more. *Maybe they will get bored and give up,* she thought.

It was different in games lessons. She had been taught how to play hockey and was pretty good at it. The girls soon found that she could be an asset to their team. Jean had organised her gang to 'go for her ankles' before they discovered how good she was. Lindy had spotted what they were trying to do and avoided being hit every time one of the girls came near her.

The game of Rounders was another success. There were no bats, the girls had to hit the ball with their fist. Lindy was good at this and she could hit the ball far around the corner into the Nun's Garden or through the gate into the road. Once the ball had been hit Lindy would walk around the playground and score a 'rounder'. This made her popular during the game's lessons, when the girls were picking the sides. But after the lesson the bullying started up again. 'Oh, you think you are so clever, hitting a few balls. You wait Pindy Lindy. We'll get you.'

Lindy, with her head down, said nothing and hoped they would lose interest.

She sat alone one day eating her lunch. Angela came and joined her. She too was not popular as she talked too much and thought she was always right. Her arguing was noted and the girls in her class avoided her. She tried sitting with girls from a lower class, but they got fed up with her bossy ways.

'I try and make friends,' she said to Lindy. 'But they don't like me.'

Lindy did not hear; she was deep in her own thoughts.

I must be strong, and not let them see how hurt I am. Perhaps I could tell Cludgy, but she might go into school and report them, and then it will get worse. Cludgy can't be by my side all the time. I don't want to tell Dad, he is so proud of me. He would be very disappointed, and I don't want that.

'I must be strong!' she said out loud.

'Strong?' said Angela. 'What are you talking about? You are strong! And clever too. My mum said.'

'Pardon, Angela,' said Lindy. 'What are you talking about? I'm not clever, I work hard.'

Angela carried on chatting without hardly taking a breath. Lindy couldn't work out what she was talking about at all. *Maybe Angela is in the same boat as me,* she thought, *no-one in her class wants to befriend her, and it's the same with me.*

Lindy looked at Angela and felt sorry for her. She smiled and the two girls sat and ate their lunch together. When Angela's mouth was full of her sandwich, Lindy took her opportunity to speak without being interrupted.

'Angela, listen to me,' said Lindy. 'Cludgy once said to me that my time would come. Be patient we'll get through this don't worry.'

'Will you be my friend?'

'I am your friend Angela.'

'Just until Barbara comes back,' said Angela

'Who is Barbara?' said Lindy.

'She's not in school, she is sick.'

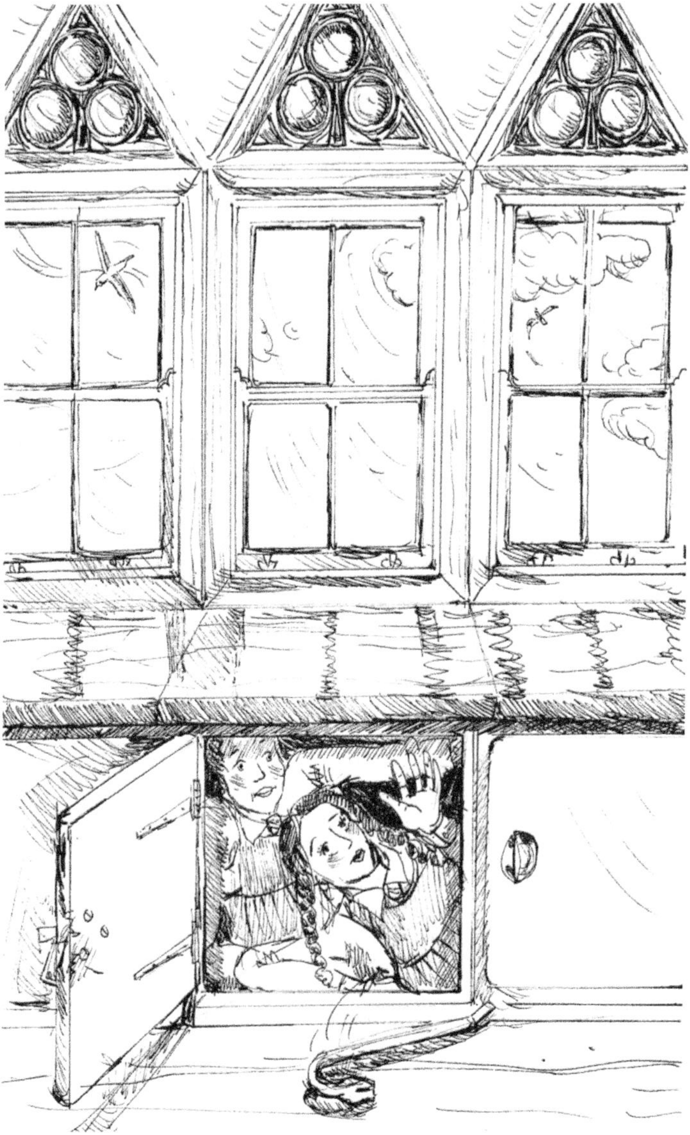

12
The History Lesson

Lindy sat at her desk next to the window on the top floor of the main building at school. She sat quietly, whilst the rest of the room were charging about.

'Do you want a pencil?' said a voice.

'Yeah, you got one?'

A pencil whizzed past Lindy's ear. It landed way beyond its target on the floor under one of the desks in the row.

The recipient of the pencil crawled about on the floor looking for it. 'Got it!' she shouted. 'Hey you rotter, it's broken!' She crawled out backwards from the under the deck banging her head as she stood up.

'Ow! I've hurt my head!' Laughter filled the room.

'Shut up you beastly rotters!' she said. 'It hurts! And the pencil is broken'

'It wasn't when I chucked it to you. Must have broken in mid-air. Just when it passed Pindy Lindy's ear!' The voice snarled and then laughed. Lindy did not react; she was used to it. There was some laughter amongst the other girls, but mostly it was a loud, 'Shush!' that was heard throughout the room.

The door to the classroom opened dramatically and banged as it hit the wall. Mrs Floyd-Brookes flounced in. Her torn, tired and worn-out university gown billowed out behind her as she charged up to the front of the class. The speed and style of entry did not mirror the girls as they dragged themselves to their feet, scraping the chairs on the floor as they did so.

'Good morning girls!' was her opening line.

'Good morning, Mrs Floyd-Brookes,' came the dreary reply from the girls.

'Sit down please,' she said.

'Now today we are going to explore the life of Henry VIII. Open your books at page 76.'

Lindy opened her rather tatty history text book which had been used by many girls in the past. The spine of the book was broken, the book lay flat. The pages had pencil marks on them, and some were loose. It gave off a strong smell of mould. *This is so old, that I wonder if Henry VIII helped write it!'* Lindy smiled as she thought to herself.

Mrs Floyd-Brookes had not made a good impression on Lindy. Throughout the lesson, she paced up and down the rows of desks. During her first circuit of the classroom, she checked the books on each desk. 'Good, you all have the same page. That's good! Good!... Good! ...Good!'

Oh goody, Lindy sarcastically thought.

'I am so glad that there are enough books to go around. You must treasure these, there are no more. There is a war on you know.'

The room remained silent. There was no response to her statement.

'Well ... never mind ...' she said. 'Let's make a start. You will see that there are some helpful notes at the foot of each page. This will be an aide memoire when you do your exams at the end of term.'

'A what?' someone said from the back of the room.

And then she started. Mrs. Floyd-Brookes did not have the most endearing voice. She droned on and on. Lindy picked up words about Spain and Catholics, but her mind was elsewhere. Looking out of the window at the blue sky she longed to be on the beach with Reggie. She pulled herself together.

I must concentrate, she said to herself. *I must concentrate! What was that? Divorce?*

As Lindy sat gazing at the blue sky, she heard a shuffle from the cupboard under the window at the side of her desk. As she looked at it the door slowly fell open, and Lindy was confronted with two smiling faces staring at her. It was her friend Angela; the other face was that of Barbara's. The girls were squashed into this small cupboard. To complete the scene, on the floor in front of them was a crowbar. Lindy stared mesmerised at the scene. What was she to do? The girls in the cupboard could not reach the door to close it. Lindy also was too far away to shut it without having to leave her seat.

Suddenly calling and shouting was heard from the playground below. Mrs. Floyd-Brookes ceased talking and got out of her seat and went over to the window to look down to the playground.

'There is something going on outside,' she said.

The class didn't wait to be asked and took the opportunity to jump up from the seats scraping their chairs on the floor again and charged over to the window to look out. Lindy did the same pushing the cupboard door shut as she went.

Mrs Floyd-Brookes opened the window and heard shouts of 'Angela! Where are you?' and 'Barbara! You need to get to your class.'

When Lindy heard this, she realised what had happened and what she had to do. She looked left and right. The girls were looking out of the window and glued to the scene acting out below them. This was Lindy's chance, she opened the door to the cupboard; Angela and Barbara untangled themselves, fell out on to the floor and headed for the door.

Lindy threw the crow bar into the cupboard, kicked the cupboard door shut and nonchalantly leant on the window sill and looked out. There were nuns and teachers frantically running around, in and out of doors and even the dormitory block was checked. They also checked in, and behind the bike shed. The search went on for a few minutes more, when one of Angela's class mates came out into the playground and spoke to Sister Theresa who was now frantic with worry. The look of relief on her face was visible from Lindy's classroom three floors up the building, that Angela and Barbara had got back into their classroom.

On the way home, Angela told Lindy, the whole story. They had discovered this cupboard which was a tunnel that went to a gallery in the church next door where they could see the whole building from a different angle. They lingered too long. They heard the bell sound and realised they were too far away from the class room to get back.

'Why was there a crowbar on the floor?' asked Lindy.

'Oh that!' said Angela. 'Yesterday we couldn't open the door, so Barbara brought it with her.'

'WHAT!' said Lindy. 'Surely if it were locked it meant that it wasn't to be opened and you weren't supposed to be there.'

'The crowbar worked really well,' Angela continued.

'Where did you go when I let you out?'

'Oh, back to the class room. We walked in as if nothing had happened. When Sister returned, we told her that we were in the lav.'

Angela gasped. 'The crowbar! Whatever has happened to the crowbar?'

'Oh, don't worry about that!' said Lindy. 'I put it in the cupboard.'

13
The Ink Blot

The bullying was getting too much. Lindy felt so alone, apart from Angela who was in a different class, it seemed that no one was talking to her. The only nice things about the school were the majority of the teachers as Lindy's work nearly always received praise. They were a bit sharp, but on the whole they didn't bully.

Apart from the rude comments, and nasty tricks of hiding her possessions so that she missed her bus on the way home, she had a sneaking suspicion that they were going through her desk and copying her work.

It was the ink blot that was the last straw. Sister Mary Magdalene, the English teacher, handed back her work.

'Your essay!' she said. 'I really don't know what to say. How you had the nerve to hand this in like that really defeats me.' She threw Lindy's book onto the desk.

Lindy picked it up and opened it up at the last page where she had been working. There was a large ink blot on the last half page of her work. There was a snigger from the back of the room.

'I couldn't read the last few lines, so I have not given you a mark.'

'But I didn't do this!' Lindy said. 'I wouldn't do this! I love English lessons and writing essays.'

'Don't answer me back!' The angry nun was now standing over her, with one finger raised, she waved it at Lindy.

'This is disgraceful behaviour, I want a whole new essay by tomorrow, AND DON'T HAND WORK IN LIKE THAT EVER AGAIN!'

'But I didn't!' Lindy repeated. Tears rushed to her eyes, but she didn't cry. Taking a deep breath, she sat up straight. *I must be strong; I will not let them see that I am upset,* she thought to herself. She knew exactly who had done this, but what she didn't know was how to deal with it. To confirm her thoughts, she heard the girls sniggering again from behind her.

'Enough!' shouted the nun. 'I will not have bad behaviour in my class!'

Back home in the safety of Smugglers Cottage Lindy sobbed. Reggie found her. He was full of the joys of spring, as his painting of Little Bridge beach had won him praise and was displayed on the wall at his new school. Lindy's head was in her hands.

'Hey Lindy!' said Reggie, 'Weren't you listening? My picture is on the wall at school!'

Lindy put her hands down, and Reggie saw her tear-stained face.

'What's up?' he said.

Reggie looked unsuccessfully for a handkerchief in his pocket. 'Sorry I haven't got one.'

'That's alright I have one, I always have one, here it is.' She produced a soggy piece of cloth from the palm of her hand.

'Gosh you have been crying!' said Reggie as he put his arm around her shoulders. 'What's happened?'

Lindy pushed her English exercise book towards Reggie, and explained the whole story. 'And I have got to do the whole essay again! Before tomorrow's lesson!'

'Nothing like that had happened at my school in Brighton or at Little Bridge School, why are they so horrid to me? I have done nothing to them at all.'

'They are probably jealous of you, because you are clever.'

'But I am not clever; well, I don't think so anyway. I have to work really hard to get good marks.'

'Perhaps that's what they are jealous of. Your marks, they don't know how hard you work.'

'They get reasonable marks, but I always beat them.'

'We need to teach them a lesson.'

'But how?' said Lindy. 'They are often looking over my shoulder at my work, and they have been in my desk. I found my rough book in a different place than I left it.'

'Ah! That's it! If they are obviously copying your work. Let's give them something to copy.'

Lindy was intrigued. 'What do you mean?'

'First things first,' said Reggie. 'You need to do the essay again!'

'I worked hard on that story,' she said between sniffs.

Reggie picked up her English essay book. 'Look the first two pages have been marked,' said Reggie, sounding very grown up and sensible. 'All you need to do is copy that, not forgetting to put in the corrections. The ink blot only hides the last three lines, that is all you have to make up.'

He sat back in his chair, put his hands behind his head and grinned. He looked very pleased with himself.

'I will make a plan of how we will pay them back. You stay here and write. Just copy your previous work.'

Lindy put her wet handkerchief back into her pocket, opened the exercise book at a fresh page and picked up her pen. 'Oh Reggie,' she said, 'Thank you so much.'

I have an idea of how we are going to catch these girls out. Leave it with me,' he said grandly, 'I'm going to go back to the cottage and get something to eat. I'm starving!'

'You are always starving.'

'I need food for thought!'

Lindy loved writing with her green fountain pen. It had been her late mother's and Lindy always felt close to her when she handled it. She had just finished writing when Reggie returned. Cludgy had made her a sandwich. Reggie carried it carefully on an enamel plate. He presented it to Lindy like a waiter. 'For Madam,' he announced. Lindy giggled.

'Have you got a plan?' Lindy asked.

'Yep! you can trust Reggie,' he said. 'We are going to catch them out at their own game. They are going to copy your work!'

'But they do that already,' replied Lindy.

'I know but the work they copy is going to be all wrong.'

'Yes ...' Lindy was curious.

How can they get English all wrong.'

'No silly, not English ... or History ... OR Geography of course.'

'But what then?'

'Maths!'

'Oh yes! I get it ... I think ... But if they copy my book, I will get them wrong too.'

'You know how you like to do a rough copy first so your book will be neat and tidy. I can't see the point to that myself. Sounds like too much hard work,' said Reggie. 'Once is enough for me, it's just a waste of ink and paper. Paper that could be used for drawing.'

'Reggie! oh do get on, what are you talking about?'

'Well, you are going to do a rough copy with all the answers wrong. Leave it in your desk, for the thieves to take and copy. You will do the correct work in your exercise book and keep that hidden until you have to hand it in.'

'That will work well,' squealed Lindy with joy. 'We have maths on Friday afternoon just before we go home. When I bring it in on Monday, I can hide my exercise book with the correct answer in my P.E. bag in the cloak room, and collect it during break. I'll carelessly leave my rough copy with all the wrong answers in my desk. Maths is the first lesson after lunch break on Monday.'

Lindy and Reggie met up at Smugglers Cottage on Saturday.

'We have got long division, long multiplication and to cap it all, we are doing percentages!' Lindy told Reggie. 'We have been given 12 problems to solve.'

'You know what percentages are I hope,' said Reggie. 'Because I don't!'

'They are parts of a whole!'

Lindy got out her rough exercise book and opened it up at the page where she had written the sums. 'Here look, we had to copy them down from the board.'

Reggie stared at the page, apart from the percentage sign itself which he thought looked quite pretty, he hadn't got a clue.

'I think I understand,' said Lindy, 'but what I can't do I will ask Cludgy or Arthur for help. They are pretty good at working things out.'

14
Retribution

With her school satchel over her shoulder Lindy hurried to the kitchen of Smugglers Cottage, carrying her after-school sandwich on a plate and a cup of tea. Reggie was already there; he was at his easel starting another picture. In front of him on the sideboard was a display of items.

'This is called a still life,' he announced proudly.

Reggie had displayed an old-fashioned copper kettle, a saucepan, cup and an old apple. 'It's supposed to be of fresh fruit and flowers, but there weren't any around, that were close enough. That's all I could find at Auntie Bee's'

Lindy's dad was at work, so the cottage was empty except for the two conspirators. She was not sure whether to involve Cludgy or her father in the plan.

'I suppose what we are conspiring to do could be seen as being horrid,' she said to Reggie.

'Nah! Don't be daft they would do the same to you ... if they could.'

'That's the point, they couldn't. From what I could see they weren't paying attention to Sister Martha. Jean was doodling and Joanna was reading a book placed on her lap.

Reggie laughed. 'This should be fun; I wish I could be there when their work is handed back to them.'

Lindy sat at the table and spread out her books. The homework the class had copied down from the board was a selection of percentages, long division and multiplication.

'The first sum to work out is 'What is 30% of 160?' said Lindy. Reggie peered over her shoulder.

'There's that sign for percentage again? I do think it is pretty!' said Reggie.

Lindy sighed and put her pen down. 'Reggie that is not being helpful.'

'Well, it is!' he insisted. … 'So, what does percentage mean?'

'Imagine one of Cludgy's cake,' said Lindy.

'Ooh yes please. What jam has she put in it?'

Lindy ignored him. 'The cake is uncut and it is the whole. If she cuts a slice for us, she will give us a percentage of the whole.'

Reggie was quiet. He was thinking of the slice .

Lindy continued. 'If she cut it in half and put that on your plate …'

'Ooh yes please,' said Reggie.

'She would have given you a half which is 50 percent. You see the cake is 100 per cent.'

'Oh, I get it!'

If she cut that half again, you would be given …

'A quarter,' Reggie butted in. 'And a quarter is half of 50 percent and that is 25 per cent. I must ask Cludgy to bake a cake and we can put that into practice!'

Lindy sighed.

'Back to the sum which was on the board. 30 percent is 30 over 100 which reverts to 3 over 10 and that has to be multiplied by the original number of 160. Then you must divide that number by 10 and multiply by three which comes out at 48. So, the answer is 48.'

'So how are you going to make that wrong?'

'Hmm,' said Lindy. 'I think I shall leave out the last calculation of multiplying by three.'

The friends beavered away at their work. Lindy continued on with her sums, Reggie got on with his picture.

She put down her pen and stretched out her arms and gave a loud and long yawn.

'Finished?' asked Reggie.

'I have completed the percentages,' she said. 'It's more difficult to write the wrong answer than to write the correct one.'

'That is,' Reggie warned, 'you have got the right answers in the first place.'

'That's true! I'll check them with Cludgy or Miss Caws up the road.' She paused, 'I don't know if I will tell her what I am doing, she may not approve.'

'What's next?' asked Reggie.

'Long division!' Lindy groaned. 'Oh, look at the first one is just too simple. I have to divide by 20, that's easy, anyone can do it.'

'Not if the numbers were not copied down correctly,' said Reggie with a wicked smile on his face.

Lindy smiled happily.

'Now let me think,' said Reggie. 'The number three could easily be mistaken for an eight, or even a five. Let's have a look.' Reggie examined Lindy's book where she had copied the sums from the board. 'The number you really need to change is the 20. It's surprizing how a zero can change into an eight with a little misplaced chalk dust.'

'Oh, Reggie you are so devious.'

Lindy changed 2359 into 2593 and divided it by 28 and then did the sum incorrectly of course. She was beginning to enjoy this.

It was the same with the multiplication. Her writing was clear and was able to be read. Here she wanted to make sure that they got all the sums correctly copied, but not correctly calculated.

She took a break before doing her real maths homework, that was to be handed in. Taking pride in writing it correctly she accurately copied her work into her rough book.

'I have changed my mind, I am going to take this to Miss Caws in Church Lane,' said Lindy.

'Are you going to tell her the truth of what you are doing?'

'Yes I think I am,' replied Lindy. 'They are bullies and I need to fight back.'

So taking her rough book she mounted her bike and took it up to her friend and tutor Miss Caws. She knocked on the door, Miss Caws opened it.

'Good afternoon Miss Caws, I am sorry to disturb you but I have a favour to ask of you,' Lindy said.

'Oh yes, what is it?' said Miss Caws.

Lindy took a deep breath, 'Well, it's like this, I am being bullied at school and ...'

'Come in my dear and tell me everything,' said Miss Caws opening the door wide as she beckoned Lindy in.

'She was directed into the sitting room, where she sat in a comfy arm chair and told her the whole story.'

'Horse droppings! In your desk! How horrid,' she said.

'And then there was the ink blot,' continued Lindy.

'So what are you going to do? And why have you come to me?'

Lindy explained Reggie's plan.

'What a good idea!' Miss Caws clapped her hands with glee. 'But my goodness I do hope it works, but what is my part in all this?'

'Could you please make sure that my homework is correct. It's percentages, long division and multiplication.'

'I think I can manage that,' she said cynically.

Lindy handed over her rough book. Miss Caws sat at her table, picked up her pen and started to mark Lindy's work.

Suddenly Miss Caws laughed. 'I think I am marking the wrong sums,' she said. 'These are all wrong!'

Lindy stood up and went to the table, she turned the page and presented her correct work to her tutor.

It took very little time for Miss Caws to go through the 12 questions.

'Well done! All correct, you certainly have mastered these percentages. And the division and multiplication are all right. Well done, I'm very proud of you. And I love the way you have answered all the other questions wrong. But how are you going to get them to the bullies?'

'I am going to write them out again on a piece of rough paper and leave it in my desk with a piece hanging out. I shall hide my rough book and maths exercise book in my shoe bag.'

Lindy couldn't wait to get back to the cottage and start work again. She cycled home at a speed that Reggie would have been proud of. He was quietly drawing at his easel. Unlike her normal procedure, Lindy threw her bike down and ran into the cottage. She pulled out her rough book from her pocket, took her maths exercise book from her bag and picked up her pen.

'Alright?' he asked.

'Yes, they are all correct.'

'Slow down, get your breath back,' said Reggie. 'You want your best work to appear in your book.'

Lindy grinned. She couldn't wait to get started.

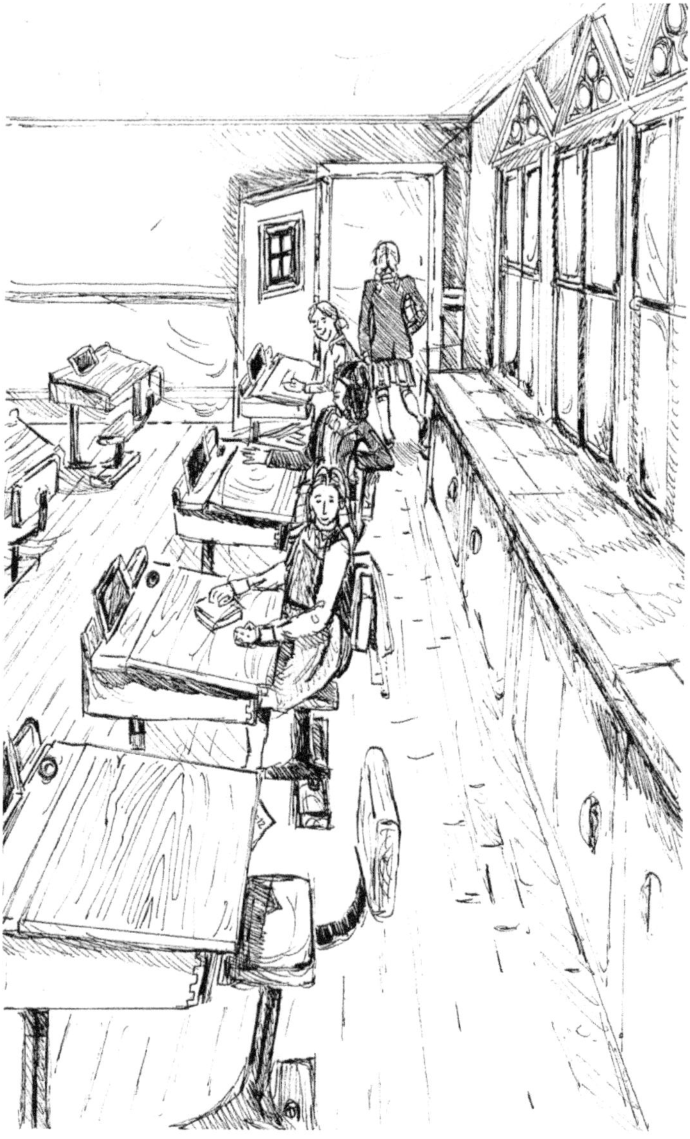

15
The Plan Is Put Into Operation

On Monday, Lindy was ready. Her hair was tidy, her school gymslip had been brushed, her tie neat and her school bag was hung over her shoulder.

'My, my, we do look tidy!' jeered Reggie.

'Lindy always takes pride in her appearance,' said Cludgy who had just put Lindy's lunch in her bag.

'Thank you Cludgy,' said Lindy. 'I'll do the buckles up.'

As the two friends left, Cludgy watched them walk up the lane. 'They are like chalk and cheese,' she muttered to herself. 'Reggie looks really scruffy, and Lindy is so neat. They don't change.'

They made their way through the lane to the bus stop.

'Are you nervous?' Reggie asked.

'Yes a little,' she replied.

'Best not talk about it on the bus in case someone hears and get suspicious.'

On the bus they talked about the possibility of riding their bikes to school and saving the bus money.

'Won't your bike be a little small for you?' said Lindy.

'I suppose so!' he said. 'I have grown a little since I first had my bike.'

'It was too small for you then,' said Lindy. 'Do you remember going up to the downs along Rolling Road.'

'We met Peggy and her boyfriend Brian up there and had to hide from the German planes. I drew a picture of that on my first day at school.'

'You were dancing in the road.' Lindy laughed.

Once off the bus, they walked together as far as the High Street, and then Reggie turned left and went to his school of art, and Lindy walked on towards the convent.

'Good luck!' said Reggie. 'I hope the plan works.'

'So do I,' said Lindy. '**Oh So do I**!'

Once inside the school premises, Lindy tried to behave as normal as possible, but she couldn't get out of her mind the subterfuge that they had planned.

She said 'Good Morning,' to various nuns and teachers and went to the cloakroom. There was no-one else in there, so keeping an eye out for other girls coming she slipped the two exercise books into her P.E. bag. She flattened out her shorts and airtex shirt and put her hockey boots side by side to make it as flat as possible. Then she pulled the string tight and tied a knot. *I'm good at undoing knots,* she thought, *I'll undo that knot quite easily.* At Reggie's advice she twisted the bag three times once it was hanging on her peg. 'That way, you will know it is has been moved or handled.' Reggie had said.

The bell rang for the girls to go to assembly. They said the usual prayers, and notices were given out.

'Some rubbish has been found in the basement air raid shelter. No-one is to go in there unless there is an air raid warning,' Reverend Mother bellowed out.

'Who would want to go down there for pleasure?' muttered someone from behind Lindy.

'I wonder what the rubbish was?' said another.

The girls trooped out to their various classrooms. The first lesson was Religious Knowledge. The class were to pick up their books and read a passage from Luke. The pupils around the room read in turn and then the nun spoke about what it meant. She then asked questions. Lindy was on tenterhooks as she hadn't been listening at all. Fortunately there were no questions for Lindy.

'Homework today is to learn that passage from Luke. Chapter 9 verses 12 to 17. And I want it word perfect.'

Thank goodness that we didn't have a passage to learn over the weekend. She thought. *I would have had trouble remembering that – WORD PERFECT.*

The second lesson was English. Happily Lindy handed in her essay that had had the ink blot.

'What's this?' asked Sister Mary Magdalene.

'It's my essay that had an ink blot on it. You told me to do it again.'

'Did I?'

'You did and here it is.'

'Put it down! Put it down!' she said impatiently. 'And go and sit down; I'll see if I have time to mark it.'

'Thank you Sister,' Lindy said meekly and went back to her desk.

Throughout the English lesson Sister Mary Magdalene explained adjectival phrases. Then during the third period, Mrs Floyd-Brookes droned on about Anne of Cleves, who was the fourth wife Henry the eighth married. Lindy felt sorry for her as she was described as plain. *I wonder how I would describe Henry the eight's appearance when he married her. He was 49 by then.*

The last lesson of the morning was Geography with Miss Barter. Lindy was now getting a little anxious. She must leave the paper with the incorrect sums on it, in her desk for the girls to find and copy. *Supposing they have already done their homework, then all my hard work will be wasted,* she thought to herself. *Going to my desk will need the room to be empty, supposing it's not, they won't be able to get the paper.*

The bell rang promptly at a quarter past 12. Despite being told to leave the room quietly there was a clatter of desk shutting and the usual scraping of chairs on the floor. Lindy did not look at the girls, but lifted her desk and put away her books, the precious piece of paper was on the top of the books. A small piece was lapping over the side. She picked up her lunch box, left the room, quickly descended the stairs, and went into the playground. Angela her friend from the lower class was already seated having her lunch. Lindy joined her.

Angela knew nothing of the plan, which was on Lindy's mind all the time. The two girls sat in silence, Lindy couldn't think of anything to say and for once Angela was quiet as she stuffed her sandwich into her mouth.

'You are quiet,' said Lindy.

'Got told off for talking too much,' Angela said in a whisper.

'Oh really, what a surprise,' said Lindy. 'What was your punishment?'

'I got sent out of the classroom,' said Angela. 'Trouble was, Reverend Mother walked by.'

'Oh dear, what did she say?'

'Nothing, she just tutted and then winked at me.'

'I think she likes you,' said Lindy.

'Thought I'd practise not saying anything,' said Angela.

'Difficult is it?' said Lindy.

'Oh yes very!'

After lunch Lindy returned via the cloakroom to collect her exercise books from her P.E. bag. Hiding them under her jumper she went to the classroom where she was last to arrive. She wanted to make sure that the girls had enough time to finish copying her work, not wanting to catch them in the act.

She opened her desk. The paper had been moved. No longer was it hanging over the side, it was placed in the middle. *They had taken the bait,* thought Lindy. She wanted to cheer out loud, but held her composure and sat up straight and still.

16
Showdown

Lindy had to wait until Wednesday before she would see the result of her plan.

Every Wednesday morning, all the girls went to Mass, so there was no religious knowledge lesson that day. Lindy liked that. It was quiet and peaceful in the church, and if the service was read in Latin, Lindy could drift off into a world of her own.

After the service the girls paraded out in single file and went straight to their class room. They had not been standing long before Mother Michael stomped in. Her heeled shoes thumped on the floor.

'We'll start with prayers,' she said sharply, 'Hail Mary …' she started before the girls were ready. They churned out the words as they always did.

'Sit down girls!' she said sharply.

Lindy did not know what was going to happen next.

'I think some of you found the homework I set difficult, so I have decided to go through it all together.'

She wrote the first problem on the board and turned around. 'Jean!' she called, 'perhaps you would like to come up to the board and do this one for the class.'

Jean's face turned white! 'I haven't got my exercise book,' she mumbled, 'I can't remember.'

'Lindy, would you do this one for me please?'

'Yes Mother,' she said and proceeded to explain how she had achieved the answer.

'Maureen! Perhaps you would like to do the next one?' Maureen's eyes and mouth opened wide.

'I haven't got my exercise book either,' she said. 'I can't remember how to do it.'

'Oh dear!' said Mother Michael, 'I'll show you how to do this one, shall I?' She turned to the board and proceeded to write, explaining as she went. The five bullies turned to each other.

'Turn around and face the board,' said the nun. 'You won't learn by looking at each other.'

In turn, she called out the rest of the five girls, Rachel was first, and then Susan and Clarissa. Each time they gave the same excuse, and another girl from the class was called to the board to complete the task.

When all 12 sums were completed on the board by the pupils, Mother Michael turned to the class and said. 'Stand up please! All of you ... **QUICKLY**!' she yelled.

There was a moment of silence. Each girl did not know what was going to happen next. Obviously, Mother Michael was angry and each girl hoped they weren't the cause of her anger.

'I am going to read the results of your homework. When you have heard your mark, you may sit down.'

'Lindy Elliot, you got them all correct, 12 out of 12. Well done.'

'Thank you,' said Lindy as she took her book.

Sarah, you too managed to achieve 12 right answers, well done.'

Mother Michael then proceeded to call out each girl's name and gave out each mark. There were six girls left, the five bullies and Bernadette, a shy small girl, who was visibly shaking as she waited her fate. Sister turned to her and smiled.

'This is your best mark to date,' she said. 'Well done you got six correct. Come and see me at the end of the lesson and I will give you some extra help when doing these calculations. Sit down Bernadette; you can be proud of your result.'

The five bullies remained standing.

Again, the room was silent except for Mother Michael's heels banging on the ground and her rosary beads rattling as she walked up and down. She went to each girl and handed out the books.

'Thank you, sister,' Jean said and moved her chair to sit down.

'No, you don't, you will remain standing.' She handed Maureen her book and Rachel was the next, then Susan and Clarissa.

'Well, well, well, you appear to have all managed to achieve the mark of zero. **ZERO**! Not a single calculation was correct. All your answers were exactly the same. How can that be?'

'We did our homework together!' said Jean.

'When did you do that?' asked Mother Michael.

'On Saturday morning. Wasn't it Maureen?'

Maureen was silent, she knew it was prudent to keep quiet.

Then out of the blue, Jean announced, 'Lindy Elliot helped us! She was very helpful!'

Lindy had not expected that accusation at all. Was her plan going to backfire? Was she in trouble too?

'Was this true Lindy?' asked Mother Michael, Lindy stood up.

'No Mother, I did not help them … no Mother … I did my homework alone, at home.'

'Yes, I know you did. I am quite sure of that.' Mother Michael smiled at her. 'Sit down my dear.'

Jean turned to Lindy, 'Yes you did!' she snarled. 'You gave us your rough copy!'

'No, I didn't **give** you anything,' replied Lindy.

'You left a piece of paper in your desk …' said Jean. Her hand went over her mouth as she realised that she had said too much.

'Did you leave the dirt and the horse droppings there too?' asked Mother Michael.

'That wasn't me! That was the others!'

There was a chorus of 'no not me!' as each girl tried to assert their innocence.

'But it was your idea,' said the lone voice of Clarissa.

'Crime doesn't pay! Does it? I have reported this to Reverend Mother, your parents are to be informed and I suggest that you go to confession as soon as you can and tell God what a wicked thing you did. Clarissa, I know you are not a catholic, but I'm sure you can discuss this with your vicar.'

'Yes Mother!' said the bullies humbly, as they sat down.

Lindy was suddenly aware of the hate these girls had for her. She had got revenge, but at what price. Revenge is supposed to be sweet. But it didn't feel like it.

At the end of the lesson Clarissa came up to Lindy.

'I am so sorry,' she said humbly. 'I have been horrid to you; will you forgive me?' She put out her hand for Lindy to shake.

Lindy was surprised, she didn't quite know what to do. She was aware that Clarissa knew about the stolen paper from Lindy's desk. However as far as the rest of the class were concerned, Lindy had not been involved in the incorrect answers to the homework. Clarissa did not want to admit she knew about the stolen paper. The class were however aware of the dirt put into her desk.

She looked at Clarissa who had tears in her eyes.

'Of course, I forgive you,' said Lindy taking her hand and shaking it. She was relieved that the hatred within the group didn't extend to all of them.

'Let's go and have lunch together,' suggested Lindy.

'Lindy,' said Clarissa, 'I honestly only joined her gang, because I didn't want to get hurt, I didn't want her to bully me.'

They sat together in the playground and ate their lunch. In between mouthfuls, they learnt all about each other. Lindy told her about her mother dying and her father being a fireman in Portsmouth, now transferred to Ryde. She told her about Cludgy, Arthur, and of course her best friend, Reggie.

Clarissa told her that her father is also a fireman. She told her how he works for Whites in Cowes and has been trained in fire fighting for the firm. Also, that she travels into school from East Cowes every day, and how if there is a raid at the end of the school day there is a bed for her to sleep in at school. Her mother is a member of the WVS.

They talked about their favourite colours, what they liked in their sandwiches, and what songs they enjoyed. At the end of lunch, Lindy had a firm friend at school.

17
The Enrolment

Auntie Bee had washed and pressed Reggie's scout uniform to perfection. He put it on, looked at himself in the mirror and felt really smart.

'You look fine!' said Auntie Bee. 'A credit to your parents.'

'Thanks!' He took another look in the mirror.

'I'm hoping that Mr Knott has a hat for me. Then my uniform will be complete.'

'Now you know your lines,' said Auntie Bee.

'I know my **promise**, Auntie Bee. It's called a promise.'

'Oh yes, I forgot! Right, off you go and enjoy the evening. I must get Uncle Robert's tea ready.'

As Reggie walked around the lane, he became aware of someone following him. He turned and saw it was Reverend Peterson.

'Good evening, Reggie,' he called out. 'Slow down. Do let me catch you up!'

'Hello Reverend, where are you going?'

'I'm going to a very special ceremony for a friend.'

'Oh, who is that?' ask Reggie.

'It's **YOU**! You are getting enrolled tonight, aren't you?'

'Why yes!' Reggie was a little surprized. He had thought it important but had not understood that this promise was important to others too.

'I know your mother and father can't be here, and that Auntie Bee is busy, so I asked Mr Knott, Skipper to you, if I could come in their place.'

'Thank you!'

'I too used to be a scout, they taught me a lot about life and people. It helped me decide to be a vicar.'

When they arrived, they discovered Miss Vaughan and Miss Brown from the Red Cross were already there, and had started to prepare the hall ready for their lesson on bleeding. Blankets and bandages were placed on the floor

'Gosh this looks exciting,' said Reverend Peterson. 'Those must be the bandages I assume. They are a bit dirty.'

The troop assembled and Skipper announced that the focus on tonight's session was how to stop bleeding.

Standing at one of the blankets the two nurses waited for the troop to gather around. 'Quick as you can, please,' said Miss Brown. 'There is a lot to do tonight.'

Miss Brown was not used to giving orders, she was a shy lady who had witnessed the results of the Great War. She had worked in a munition factory making weapons for the soldiers to kill and maim with. As the war progressed and the men returned, Miss Brown as a member of the Red Cross saw the results of war and injuries that the weapons inflicted on the bodies of these young men. These weapons were similar to the type of weapon she was making.

These young men had joined up for a bit of an adventure. But now she saw men in wheel chairs, men with limbs missing, scarred faces and bodies. In 1917, as soon as she could she left the factory and went to work on the land as a member of the newly formed Land Army. She toiled on farms helping to feed the nation.

Miss Brown never married; her boyfriend did not return from the Somme. He was blown to bits; his body was never found. She hadn't known him long when he died, only finding out about his death from reports of another lad from the village. In casual conversation, she asked after him. She never found out who he was, he just said 'Oh, he died too.' No-one knew the pain and shock that she was suffering, she hid it well and threw herself into her war work.

It was important to her to help in this war. Too old at 64 to work on the land she volunteered as a Red Cross nurse. Safe in the knowledge that she was helping the sick and wounded, and not being part of the killing process. Now Miss Brown was helping others to learn how to help the injured.

The boys shuffled into a group on the floor ready to watch the demonstration. Miss Vaughan stood tall and slim; Reggie gazed at her adoringly. *Lovely,* he thought. In contrast, Miss Brown was short and dumpy.

'Now I need a volunteer please!' she announced. There was a pause as the boys looked around at anything other than at her. 'Now come on I won't bite.'

Skipper rose to his feet and was about to volunteer someone, when the vicar stood up. 'I'll do it,' he said. There was a slight sound of giggling which ceased immediately when their leader turned and glared at them. They had never imagined someone so upstanding and serious as their vicar, rolling about on the floor being bandaged up.

Miss Brown was a little surprised. 'Right ... Thank you Vicar ... Wo... wo ... would you please lie down on the blanket. ... please,' she stuttered. She picked up a bandage which had been rolled up, and promptly dropped it on the floor. It opened out and rolled away.

The boys laughed again, but this time it was allowed. Peggy picked it up and proceeded to roll it up again.

When the laughter subsided the troop settled and Miss Brown explained what she was going to do. There was one more difficulty she had to overcome, and that was because it was a cut on the foot, she was going to have to take his shoe off. 'Oh, please don't have a hole in your sock,' she muttered to herself. 'That will cause another bout of laughter.' It was alright, Reverend Peterson's socks were perfect. Miss Brown breathed a sigh of relief.

She couldn't quite bring herself to take off his sock. Her branch of the Red Cross was heavily staffed by women. Handling bodies in training were all women, not men. This was going to be difficult. She put dressing on the imaginary wound first, and then bandaged the foot over the sock.

'Wouldn't you take the sock off first?' said one of the assembled audience. This was getting all too much for her.

Miss Brown continued to bandage the foot. 'Err … err… err' was all that she could utter.

Peggy Vaughan stood up to rescue her friend, who was getting more and more flustered. 'That's a very good question,' she said. 'If the bleeding was excessive, taking the sock off may disturb the wound. We are giving them first aid. The aim is to stop the flow of blood. Once he had arrived at the hospital or to a first aid post, then I would consider taking the bandage off and removing the sock. There would be help from more senior staff. I would wash the wound and reapply a fresh bandage.'

'What should you do with the leg once you have finished bandaging it?' said Miss Brown.

There was silence again. Suddenly Reggie lifted his arm in the air. 'Raise it,' he said. 'My dad told me!'

'You are right!' said Miss Brown. 'But why?'

'Because fluid doesn't travel up hill.'

'Right again. Well done,' said Miss Brown.

Now you should have a dressing and a bandage by each blanket. Please get into your groups and take it in turn to bandage each other's foot.'

'Shall we leave the sock on or take it off?'

The two nurses sighed. 'It's up to you.' they both said in unison. Then they caught each other's eye and started to giggle. They disappeared into the small room at the side of the stage. Once composed they returned and went to each group to give them pointers.   Skipper and Reverend Peterson went to each group and gave encouraging words

It took an hour to get through the exercise of controlling the bleeding from a cut foot. Each boy had to be a casualty and then each boy had to be the first aider and bandage up the foot. After they finished, they folded each blanket, rolled up each bandage, put them in the practice first aid box and put on their socks and shoes.

Skipper stood up and called out. 'Troop! Alert!'

The boys in their patrols made a circle. 'Wolf Patrol! You are responsible for the flag; would you collect it and bring the flag pole.'

Two boys collected the pole and placed it at the side of their leader. They tied the Union flag to the rope, making sure it was the right way up. The ceremony was about to start, so the flag was raised and Reggie walked forward with Peter his patrol leader. Reggie stood in front of the flag and Skipper. 'This is Reggie Mitchell Skipper, and he wishes to make his promise to become a scout.'

'Thank you, Peter,' said Mr Knott.

Reggie suddenly felt very self-conscious and a little nervous. *This is daft he thought, I can do this!*

'Would you like to make your promise?'

'Yes sir,' whispered Reggie, then he cleared his throat and repeated. 'Yes sir!'

'Take hold of the end of the flag. Troop! Salute.'

Reggie put his hand up smartly and held his salute and he was about to start to speak when that awful wailing sound started. It was an air raid warning.

'Right boys you know the routine, out to the air raid shelter. Don't forget to collect a blanket on the way.'

'Those boys who have extra responsibilities,' Mr Knott called out. 'Off you go and good luck!'

The younger boys trouped out of the exit door picking up a folded blanket on the way. Reggie watched as Peter his patrol leader left to go to the ARP post. Ronald had the shortest route to take to get to the Fire post as it was next door in the house down the slope. The troop boasted two first aiders, David and Malcolm, fortunately they had their bikes as they needed to get to the first aid post near the church. Although the two nurses mounted their bikes at the same time the two boys were quicker and they got to the post before them. Henry was a member of the Home Guard. He too had a bike and rushed out of the door mounted his bike and cycled as fast as he could as he had the furthest to go. Their post was at the Quays.

Reggie was in awe of the boys rushing off to do their duty. How he envied them. *I'm going to do something useful being a scout.* He vowed to himself.

'Reggie!' shouted Mr Knott, 'Reggie! stop daydreaming. Quickly as you can, get to the shelter. Pick up a blanket it may get chilly later on.'

He grabbed a blanket and ran to the shelter.

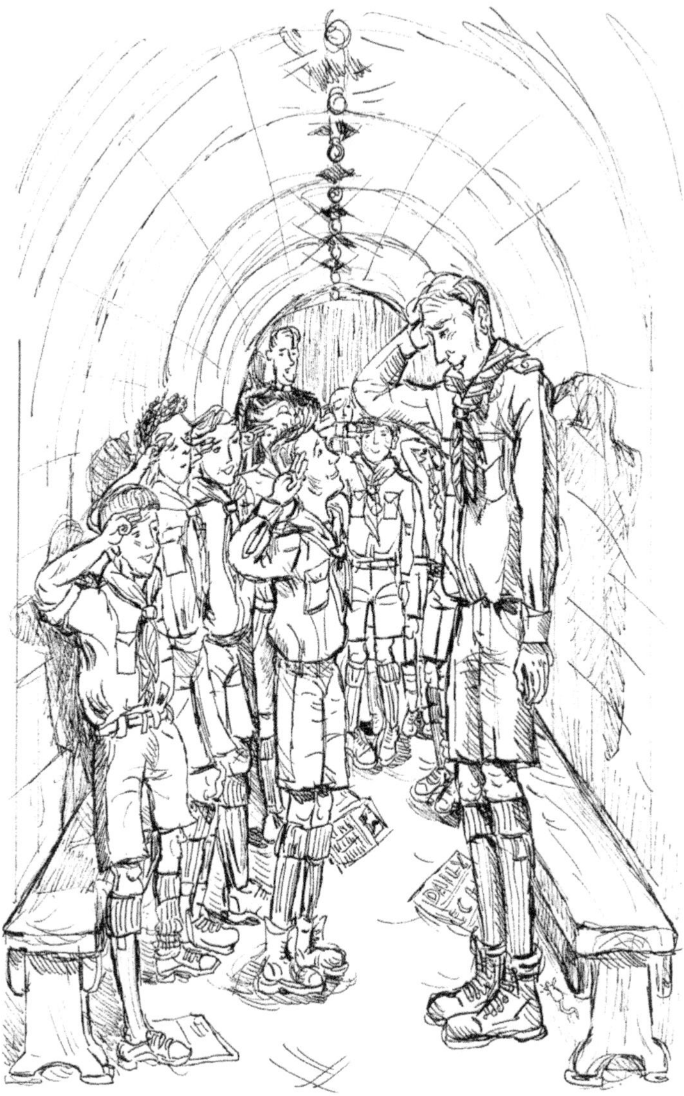
DAILY

18
The Explosion

The hall's Air Raid shelter was long. It had been set deep in the earth, there were benches running the whole length on both sides, most of the boys were seated on their folded blankets. To keep their feet dry duck boards were lined up along the plain earth floor.

Reggie joined the bench at the end. After a little shuffling the boys settled down. Reverend Peterson was at the far end of the shelter, Skipper was at the other by the door.

'A scout whistles and is cheerful under all difficulties!' said Skipper. His words were not heard as planes flew overhead. 'A scout whistles and is cheerful under all difficulties!' he repeated. The boys looked at him. 'We will start with a smile, and then we will whistle.'

The boys whistled, Reggie puckered his lips and blew. No sound came out, just spit, but his inability to make any noise was not noticed as from the far end a beautiful clear whistle was heard. It was Reverend Peterson. The boys stopped and he continued whistling a tune.

The captive audience sat still and listened until he had finished. Then they clapped enthusiastically. 'Who knows what that tune was?' asked Skipper.

Reggie raised his arm. 'Yes Reggie, what is it?' '

'It was 'Somewhere over the Rainbow;' I know I saw the film.'

'Thank you, Reverend Peters, that was most entertaining,' said Skipper. 'I think he deserves his entertainer's badge. Who else is going to entertain us whilst we are here.'

Between the noise of the planes flying over, there followed many camp fire songs. Reggie's favourite was Ging Gang Goolie, because it broke into two parts, with half the group singing 'Oompa, Oompa' and the rest the tune.

After a few songs there were some individual turns. A choir boy sang the 23rd Psalm, another performed a music hall song taught to him by his granny. Two boys from the same school did a recitation from Shakespeare.

Reggie put his hand up. 'I would like to do an impression,' he announced grandly.

'Right you are, Reggie,' said Skipper. 'What or who are you going to impersonate.'

'It's an owl!' he said in a serious tone, and then he paused. There was a snigger from some boys who knew Reggie from Little Bridge School and knew what was coming. 'It's not an ordinary owl. I am going to impersonate the very rare back to front owl.'

Reggie turned his back on his audience, put his hands under his arms and proceeded to flap them as he walked backwards saying 'Oooh Twit! Oooh Twit.' Laughter filled the shelter, the more they laughed the more Reggie carried on. The boys got up and joined in, they stood on the benches and flapped their wings and called out, 'Oooh Twit, Oooh Twit'. Eventually exhausted Reggie stopped and gave a bow. They all clapped. The last to stop laughing and clapping was Reverend Peterson who continued long after the others had finished. He got an extra round of applause.

'I have an idea,' said Mr Knott. 'Your enrolment ceremony was ruined by the raid; how would you like to make your promise here and now. No-one has ever said their promise in an air raid shelter.'

Reggie smile, he liked that idea.

Leaving their benches, the boys stood to attention, some stood on the benches so that they could all see Reggie.

'Are you willing to make your promise now?'

'Yes,' said Reggie. He cleared his throat, waited for the airplanes to pass overhead and then he started. 'I promise to do my best, to do my duty to God and the King, to help other people at all times, and to obey the Scout Law.'

Mr Knott produced a scarf from his pocket, placed it around Reggie's neck and slipped the leather woggle over the two ends and pushed it up.

'I made this one especially for you,' he said and then he stopped and waited for more planes to fly over. 'I would have liked you to have made it yourself but couldn't find the time. Perhaps you would like to make one yourself, we could give it to the next new boy who joins the scouts.'

'Yes sir, I would like that.'

'Troop!' he shouted. There was a pause … 'Alert!' Mr Knott called out giving the instruction. The boys stood still.

'Now settle down,' Skipper continued. I think we are going to be here a while. Get as comfy as you can. Does anyone have a camp fire story to tell?' Reverend Peterson put up his hand.

'Oh good,' said Skipper, glad that he didn't have to remember one of the endless stories he had been told throughout his years as a scout.

The air raid shelter became quiet. Reverend Peterson recounted a story about an unexpected visitor to Little Bridge church. In it were owl hoots, creaky hinges, ghostly singing, and lots of footsteps. The boys were transfixed. All was silent when suddenly Skipper said, 'There have been no planes over head for 30 minutes now, we should hear the all clear pretty soon. Then we can get these boys back home to bed.'

'Right! A lot of them are falling asleep anyway,' said Reverend Peterson. He continued his story, 'And the key to the vestry turned and the door creaked open. There standing in the doorway was …

At that point there was an almighty explosion. Through the door at the end, light poured in to the shelter. Then there was a pitter patter sound of something landing on the top of the shelter and the ground. 'That can't be rain, can it?' said Reverend Peterson. He strode towards the exit.

'No don't go out, stay here, there may be more bombs. They tend not to drop bombs one at a time,' warned Mr Knott. 'Wait a little longer!'

'Alright! I'll wait.' said the vicar. 'Stay strong. Stiff upper lip, eh?'

Some of the boys did not have the resilience and the stiff upper lip of the two men who were peering out of the door. Reggie however recognised the younger boys' fear, as he too was a little afraid, but he was one of the older boys here, so he felt he had to be an example. He went over to them.

'Look we are alright!' he said. 'No-one is hurt. We are going to be alright. Chin up.'

The boys settled again and it was all eerily quiet. A quietness that would have suited the Reverend Peterson's story.

'It must have been an unexploded bomb going off, that had been dropped during a previous raid,' suggested Skipper. It sounded as if it came from the field behind the hut. When the all clear is sounded we'll go and have a look.'

After what seemed like a long wait, the single tone of the all clear sounded and the members of the 1st Little Bridge scouts breathed a sigh of relief.

'I'll go around the back and see if I can see anything,' said Reverend Peterson.

'Thanks,' said Skipper. 'Stay well back, don't go too close. I'll get the boys back into the scout hut and organise how we are to get them home.' He turned around and faced the troop.

'Right boys!' he said. 'Fold up your blankets and we will return to the hut altogether. Help each other won't you. Patrol leaders or seconds put your arm up high when your patrol is ready.'

The troop walked back by the light of the stars and moon to the hut. Mr Knott opened the door and walked in. There was no light, he tried the switch. Reggie rushed forwards, 'The blackouts Skipper,' said Reggie.

'Thanks Reggie, but you needn't have worried, the power is off.'

As Reggie and Mr Knott walked further into the hall, he felt his feet crunch on something on the floor.

'Sir, there is something under my feet. It's crunchy.'

As their eyes adjusted to the dim light, they could just see that there was glass strewn all over the floor. Mixed with the glass were big bits of mud.

'Reggie! stop the boys from coming any further. I don't want them tripping and cutting themselves.

By the light of the moon coming through the broken windows, Mr Knott called 'Troop!' he paused before giving the second command, and then said, 'Alert!' Still at the back of the hall, the boys lined up.

'We are going to walk you all home. Does anyone turn left at the top of the road?' No-one answered. He waited. 'That's fine! So, I want you to walk in twos, and we will start our journey along the main road with Reverend Peterson at the back and I'll be at the front. Any questions?'

There were none. 'Too tired,' said the vicar.

'Terry and William, you both live near the pub, so that will be our first stop. Our next stop is for Lloyd and Paul. You both live near the cemetery.'

'You sound like a bus conductor,' said the Reverend Peterson.

'Yes, I do,' said Skipper.

The walking bus worked well. At each stop, the Reverend Peterson or Skipper took the boys to their front door and then returned to the group. Some mothers were at their front door anxiously looking out for their sons. One came down the road and took four boys and dropped them off at their houses before returning to her home.

Reggie was the last one left. I'll walk Reggie back to the cottage by the church knowing it as well as I do. You go on home.'

'Thanks for coming tonight,' said Skipper. 'You have been a great help.'

'I only meant to stay a short while to see Reggie's enrolment.'

The three of them separated at the bottom of Little Bridge Hill, and Reggie and Reverend Peterson walked along the dark lane.

'What was in the vestry that was so scary?' asked Reggie.

'Scary? What are you talking about?'

'Your story about the singing and funny noises in Little Bridge Church.'

'Oh that! It was Cludgy cleaning the brass, she always sings when she does that job.'

Reggie was a little disappointed with the conclusion of the tale.

They had just turned towards the church when Reggie saw Auntie Bee and Robert coming up the lane to meet them.'

Reggie ran towards them and straight into Auntie Bee's open arms.

'I was a little worried Reverend.' she said. 'We heard an explosion.'

'Oh that, we thought it must be a UXB,' said Reverend Peterson. 'We reckoned that it was an unexploded bomb that went off in the field behind the hall.'

I'm alright. See!' said Reggie. 'I'm a scout now! I was enrolled in the air raid shelter during a raid!'

'You are not going to forget your enrolment Reggie, are you,' said Reverend Peterson. 'Neither am I.'

19
Waste Not Want Not

It was the turn of the Eagle Patrol to take the hand cart around the village to collect any salvage. The booty they collected consisted mainly of old newspapers as well as tin cans and worn-out clothes. The old saucepans and oven trays were destined to become aeroplanes. The boys had witnessed dog fights over the island, so loading these onto the cart were real worthwhile trophies.

The patrol leader was Peter. He asked for volunteers and Reggie willingly agreed to join him. The other boys had other activities to attend to. A couple were gardening with Arthur, and the others were helping to clean an old house that was to be occupied by a bombed-out family from Newport.

Peter and Reggie met by the post office in Little Bridge. Their plan was to take the cart up Little Bridge Hill and start at the top. They were just passing the village shop when Mrs Smithers called out from the house further up the hill.

'Here you are lads, I've some rags for you. They had been used for cleaning but are so thin that they are of no further use to me.'

'Thanks,' said Peter.

'Oh yes, and I have this old coat which is too small for my Verity now, she is growing so fast. Will you take it?'

'Yes, I'll pass it on to the WVS they have a stack of second-hand clothes that can be reused. I will add this to their collection.'

Half way up the hill, Mrs. Bennett came out of the house and waited in the front garden.

'I've got Mr Bennett's newspapers for you,' she called. 'He likes to keep a record of the happenings. He marks them up on his map in the dining room.'

'How interesting,' said Peter. He was being polite, as he was dreading being asked into the house to admire the map.

'Yes, he likes to keep abreast of the times,' Mrs Bennett continued. 'Some of the papers have been cut, as Mr Bennett has saved the reports of important events.' Mrs Bennett had neatly piled up the papers and tied them up with string.

'Thank you, Mrs Bennett. Must get on! Bye!' said Peter hurriedly thus escaping the visit to admire Mr Bennett's map. 'Hey Reggie! look after the string, that is always useful.'

Carelessly Reggie threw the pile of papers onto the cart. It landed face down. Reggie suddenly noticed the small strip cartoon of Jane. He paused, beckoned Peter and together they leant forward to take a closer look. Jane was scantily dressed throughout.

They were transfixed by what they saw. Mrs Bennett noticed and went closer to see what they were looking at.

As soon as she realised, she pushed the boys away, and turned the pile the other way up to reveal the first page of the Daily Mirror. With their heads down the boys cleared their throats, thanked Mrs Bennett again and went on their way.

At the top of the hill, they turned right and saw the housekeeper from the big house running down to the road carrying three saucepans. The pans clanked together as she ran.

Reggie's eyes lit up. *Saucepans means Spitfires!* he thought.

'Peter! Reggie! Here you are, something for the cart. Do you want these?' she gasped. 'The mistress of the house says that we must give up some aluminium for the war effort. I have been through the pans and came up with these. We have plenty, so they won't be missed. I chose the ones in the worst condition!'

'They look perfect!' said Peter. 'Thank you very much! I am sure they are just what is needed.'

They trekked all morning, up and down the lanes, collecting all sorts of items. Their truck was almost full when they ended up in a road at the north end of Ryde, where there were terraced houses belonging to the not so wealthy.

Some of the houses in the block were just rubble, they had been made safe, but were uninhabitable. These houses had been destroyed by a German land mine in a raid in June.

'The mines are attached to parachutes and they float down to the ground.' said Peter. 'Or whatever is in the way of them reaching the ground.'

Reggie stared horrified. 'Then some people died here.'

'Oh yes, 11 and some were children.'

'These enormous bombs cause an equally enormous explosion which annihilated the school,' continued Peter.

They passed the Church, which had not escaped being damaged. The roof of the side aisle was torn off.

'There were in fact two mines; one failed to explode.'

'Gosh what more damage would have been caused if that one had exploded too.'

Peter and Reggie's attention was diverted when they saw Mrs Thomas coming out of one of the houses waving a small saucepan.

'Hey boys!' she called out. 'I've got a pan I can give you if you want it?'

Peter and Reggie turned and pulled the cart towards her.

'Hello boys,' she said. 'You look exhausted. My! my! haven't you collected a lot of salvage. Would you like a drink,' she said. 'I bet you are thirsty and tired. I can offer you a drink of squash, some tea or water.'

'We are a bit tired,' Peter replied.

The boys followed Mrs Thomas to the kitchen. Reggie looked at the bottle of squash in her hand which was nearly empty. 'I'd like a drink of water please.'

'So would I,' said Peter. '

'Now. A pan. Which one is the best to give you, I'll choose the worst,' she laughed. 'This one is so battered that it won't stand on the stove anymore unless it has something in it. I'll give you that one with pleasure.'

Mrs Thomas held out a very bent pan, with various dents in it. 'The handle is loose as well and the bottom isn't flat anymore, hence it falls over when it's empty.'

'That's just what we need,' said Peter.

The boys finished their water, and thanking Mrs Thomas they left. Reggie ran in front to the cart and jumped on the back. He dug down under the rags and paper and found the three pans the hired help at the house at the top of Little Bridge Hill had given them. He picked them up and without saying any more, he jumped down, ran back into the house and swapped the last two equally battered pans for the three good ones.

'Is that alright with you Mrs Thomas?'

'Ooh yes,' she said. 'My! Aren't they lovely. Many thanks. But these look new, should I really be taking these?'

'I call that a straight swap,' reasoned Reggie. 'You have given us your pans, and I have given you these.' With that Reggie turned, called out, 'Bye!' waved and ran back to the cart.

'What have you done?' asked Peter when Reggie had returned.

'We haven't lost anything and we did gain two pans. The aluminium is what is needed, and bashed pans have the same value as smart ones,' Reggie paused.   '... AND Mrs Thomas is in need of decent saucepans.'

20
Being a Scout

Reggie was really getting into the swing of things. He envied the other boys for their badges they had sewn on their right sleeve. He told everyone what his plans were. He was going to do all the badges. *So many that there won't be enough room on my shirt to sew them,* he thought to himself, *I am going to get an armful. I shall work so hard, that they will find it difficult to keep up with me. I must choose badges that will be useful to the war effort though.*

One hot day, Lindy was sitting with Reggie on the beach, when he announced, 'I am determined that now that I am a scout, I am going to do lots of badges. Shall I tell you which ones?'

'I'm sure, no I am positive, that you have told me before. Haven't you told everyone in the village? But you are going to tell me again, whether I want to listen or not! Aren't you?'

'Oh, Lindy don't be like that, be interested … please.'

'Oh, alright then, I'm listening.'

Lindy put on a sweet contorted smile and stared directly at Reggie's face.'

'What are you looking at me like that for?' said Reggie.

'I'm listening! … and I am concentrating, said Lindy. 'well, get on with it then.'

'Right you are. I have decided to start with five badges.'

'Only five?' said Lindy sarcastically.

'Yes, I will tackle the rest when I have finished these. I am going to do the First Aid badge, Gardener's, Dispatch Rider, Artist's, and most important of all the Fireman's badge.'

'That is a lot of work,' said Lindy. 'And you have to consider your school work; you must not let yourself get behind there. Your Dad won't be pleased if you do.'

'That's what Reverend Peterson said when I told him which badges I wanted to do.'

'You have chosen a lot, and have told a lot of people, wouldn't it be best if you started working on them one at a time?'

'Lindy, you sound more like Auntie Bee every day. I can manage, I have it all worked out.'

'Right!' said Lindy. 'There are only 24 hours in a day, you know. In that 24 hours you have to eat, go to school, do some chores for Auntie Bee, do your school homework and then you have to sleep as well!'

Reggie thought for a while, 'I know, I know, don't keep going on, I can do it.' He put his hand into his pocket and produced his well-thumbed small booklet. He opened it up and bent the book back at the beginning of the section on Proficiency Badges. 'Look here are the badges and what I have to do to pass them. Firstly, there is the artist's badge.'

Lindy sighed. She was finding it increasingly difficult to muster up any fresh enthusiasm for these badges, but managed to say, 'That should be easy, you draw and paint all the time.'

Lindy looked over Reggie shoulder at the book. 'There is a lot of text printed under that badge. What else do you have to do to pass?' asked Lindy.

'Well ...' Reggie paused.

'Let me see!' said Lindy as she took the book, and read out loud. "Demonstrate interest, practice and proficiency in some form of one of the following ..."

'What?' said Reggie. 'What is profishi ...sence?

'Proficiency,' Lindy corrected him. It means your ability to do the picture or whatever you choose to do. I would say that you are very proficient.'

'Proficient,' Reggie repeated. 'Really, you think I am proficient?' Reggie was flattered.

Lindy read on silently. 'You could do modelling, or carving too.'

Modelling?' said Reggie. 'You mean with plasticine. I don't think we have any.'

'Won't they have some at school.'

'Yes, but it's old stuff, it has been used and used and all the colours are mixed in together.'

'That doesn't matter, it is the shape you make with it that they will look at.'

'Ah!' said Lindy. 'There is a little more to do than just paint a picture or make a model.'

'What?' said Reggie. He leant over and grabbed the booklet. 'What else do I have to do?'

'Give me the book back and I'll tell you.' Lindy took the book. 'It's not just creating your masterpiece; you have to name three famous people who have created some work in the style you have chosen.'

Reggie looked down trodden.

'You didn't expect it to be easy, did you?' said Lindy. 'You did! Didn't you?' Lindy looked at her friend sympathetically. 'You can ask other people you know.'

He perked up. 'You mean like the vicar.'

'Yes, or Cludgy, Arthur, or Auntie Bee,' said Lindy. 'Or your teacher at school.'

'Oh, that's good. And I can do anything I want really. I fancy doing a bit of modelling. It won't matter what it looks like, I could call it abstract. You know like Cludgy said.'

'But you like your work to look right.'

'I know, but there are some pretty weird statues, and models that look like nothing at all.'

'I have an idea!' said Lindy. 'You know Peggy's fiancé, Brian? Well his aunt, had a brother who was a sculptor, he died last year, you could ask her for names of people in the art world.'

'Yes, the Vicar told me about her. He said that she may know other famous artists. I'll go and knock on her door and ask then.'

'No, I suggest you speak to her after church, or talk to Peggy and ask her to introduce you. She is an old lady with old fashioned manners.'

They returned to the book. 'Let's look at what else are you planning?'

'I hope they are not as hard as the artist badge. I thought that one was going to be easy.'

Lindy turned the page and found the First Aid Badge.

'That one **is** easy,' said Reggie. 'Peggy Vaughan and Mrs Brown are teaching us on Tuesdays. Now that is one of the useful badges. Useful for war work. I mean.'

'Isn't the Artist Badge useful?' asked Lindy.

'No not really, in first aid, I can help people, and even save a life, but … you just look at art.'

Lindy couldn't answer that; she decided to go on to the next one. 'Gardener!' she announced

'That's pretty simple,' he said confidently. It's all about cultivating a piece of land. I did a lot of gardening when I was working with Arthur, after that business with the catapult.'

'Ah yes, that incident with the catapult and the policeman's greenhouse.'

'Alright don't go on Lindy!' said Reggie.

'Do you know the names of 12 plants?'

'Yes, I do!'

'Well name them then!'

'Potatoes, tomatoes, beans, peas, strawberries, raspberries, blackberries ... shall I continue?' Reggie said boastingly.

'Blackberries grow wild, you can't name them as something you cultivated.'

Another dose of silence occurred. Reggie leaned back on the sand; he lay still opening his mouth periodically as if to say something. He'd rise up slightly on his elbows and then say 'No', and drop back again, shut his eyes and delivered another silence. Lindy decided she was not going to ask! She raised her eyebrows and sighed. After a while, Lindy had had enough.

'Reggie Mitchell, what's the matter?' Another silence ensued. Then as if his body was struck by lightning, he sat up.

'Can I borrow your bike, Lindy?'

'What?

'Can I borrow your bike?' he repeated.

'Yes, but what for?'

'I'll keep it clean, well-oiled and in good working order.'

'Reggie, what do you want it for?'

'I'll look stupid on my bike; my legs are too long now.'

'Reggie, where are you going to ride to on my bike?'

'All over the place, I'll need it for taking important documents all over the island. My bike is far too small. PLEASE Lindy let me borrow your bike.'

'When do you want it?'

'Don't know!'

'Alright how long will you need it?'

'Depends how long the air raid is. Let's say as long as the incident is happening.'

'So, you only need it during air raids or other incidents.'

'That is when I have passed the test, and I will also need it for the test,' said Reggie humbly. 'Please, please!'

'What test?' asked Lindy.

'Oh, didn't I mention that, it's for my Despatch Riders badge. I have to own a bike in good working order, and yours is and ... mine isn't.'

'Alright then, because it is for the war effort. But I shall be checking on my bike and making sure you are looking after it properly.'

'I will, ... I promise, I will.' Reggie face was contorted into an expression of pleading.

'I see there is a Fireman's badge. How will you have enough time to do it all,' said Lindy. 'There's lots to learn in this one.'

'Oh, that one!' said Reggie. 'Skipper has arranged with your dad and the Ryde fire station to do some training with the men there.'

'So when?' asked Lindy.

'When what?' said Reggie.

'When are you borrowing my bike?'

'When I do the test.'

'When is the test?'

'Not for ages silly. I have all this other stuff to do.'

Lindy felt a pang of jealousy. Reggie was going to work closely with her dad. How she would have loved to do the same. But she was a girl and it was not permitted. She would only be allowed to work in the Fire Brigade's telephone switch board and even receive messages, but not work on the fire engine, or hold a hose directing it towards a fire.

'Women are not strong enough,' William told his daughter. 'Anyway, you are to be a young lady. The work would be far too hard and heavy for you.'

Lindy who was still a little taller than Reggie, thought this unfair. 'I am just as strong as Reggie; I am sure I could do the job,' she told her father.

He was not persuaded.

21
A Real Emergency

Cludgy stood at the kitchen table, the sleeves of her dress were wet and strands of her curly hair dripped over her face.

'What happened to you?' asked Lindy.

A pile of washing lay on the floor. Lindy leant down to pick a pillow case up and realised that it was very wet as was the rest of the pile.

'Leave it there please,' she said. 'I was tending my tomatoes on the allotment, when rain suddenly fell from the sky. I rushed to the walled garden to get the washing in, but I was too late. I grabbed a sheet and unpegged it from the line. Then to make matters worse I dropped it on the ground. It landed in a newly dug bed.'

'You are soaking too!' remarked Lindy.

'I know. It was a short shower, but long enough to get me totally soaked as well as the washing. I must get changed into something dry.'

Together they picked up the sheet, and held it out. A large muddy stain appeared in the middle.

'Oh no,' said Cludgy, 'I'll have to wash it again, it's filthy.' She separated it from the other washing and left it in a heap on the floor.

Just as Cludgy went outside to collect the large galvanised washing tub, Lindy picked up further pillow cases, and two towels which had suffered the same fate.

'The sun went in,' continued Cludgy. 'but I was so engrossed in my tomatoes that I did not notice the black cloud looming. Bother! Oh bother!"

'Sorry Cludgy, but there is more to do.' She held up the pillow cases and towels.

Cludgy sighed, 'I can't blame this on the war, can I?'

'May I help?' Lindy asked.

'Could you please go around to Auntie Bee's, tell her what has happened and ask if I could come and use her mangle. I will have to dry this indoors and a good squeeze through the mangle will prevent an excess of drips on my floor.'

'The weather may change,' Lindy said with a smile, 'the sun may come out and be just in time to dry your washing.'

Lindy rushed next door and told Auntie Bee who was more than willing to go to Cludgy's aid. Reggie rushed to Cludgy's kitchen to see the drama of the muddy sheets.

He spotted the large double sheet with the muddy stain. 'Oh gosh, that is awful!' he said. 'It'll take you ages to do that washing again. Will the muddy stain **ever** come out? It looks really terrible. Anyway, look on the bright side, it's in the middle of the sheet so it won't show with blankets over it. Will you have to boil them again on the stove, or are you going to leave them to soak?'

'Reggie that is not helpful,' said Cludgy. 'Yes, it should come out. I do know what I am doing.'

Auntie Bee and Lindy joined them in the kitchen, which was beginning to look like a laundry as apart from the muddy sheet, there was a basket of clothes to do as well.

The two ladies set to work. They picked up the large washing tub and put it on the range. Auntie Bee filled a large saucepan with water from the tap, took it over to the range and poured it into the tub. Cludgy added some logs to the fire. Lindy and Reggie joined in. They each took a sauce pan from the rack. Reggie was first to fill it up at the sink and went to the tub, poured it in as Lindy filled hers and did the same. They were followed by Auntie Bee and Cludgy.

Some soap powder was added to the tub and Cludgy stirred the mixture with a large wooden spoon. Then the two ladies picked up the sheet and together they loaded it into the washing tub.

'It had to be my large double sheet! Just my luck.' Cludgy said. 'Why couldn't it have been Lindy's single one?'

Lindy and Reggie stood around watching. The two ladies were so adept at working together they knew exactly what to do to help each other. After they had loaded the towels and the other pillow cases into the tub, they sat down for a rest.

Suddenly Cludgy sprung to life. 'Oh, my goodness,' she said, 'I've the shopping to do as well. It never rains but it pours.'

'We can do the shopping,' said Lindy. 'Can't we Reggie?'

'Of course, we can,' said Reggie rather glad they didn't have to help with the washing.

'I've done the list, it's on the sideboard together with the ration books.'

'Is there much to do?' asked Lindy.

'No, but you will need at least two bags,' said Cludgy. Start at the top of the town at the Health Food Shop and work down to the green grocers and the butchers. I'm afraid you will find the usual queues.

'That's alright,' said Lindy. It's stopped raining and is turning out to be a nice day, look the sun is out.'

'It is now!' said Cludgy grudgingly. 'If the sun had shone this morning, and the rain hadn't come, I wouldn't be doing all this washing again!'

Lindy and Reggie took Cludgy's wicker basket, two bags, purse, money and the ration books. There were four books, one each for Cludgy, Arthur and Lindy's father and one for Lindy.

'Take care,' Cludgy called out, as the children walked up the lane.

Lindy had the purse put away in her convent school blazer she was wearing. Reggie had no serviceable pockets, the two in his shorts had holes in them.

On the bus to Ryde, Lindy paid the fares.

'I'm glad we are doing the shopping,' said Reggie, 'I didn't fancy doing the washing. All that lugging and heaving wet sheets, not my idea of fun.'

'Yes, you are right. I wonder if they will have to scrub the muddy stain.'

They got off the bus by the large church on the corner and proceeded to make their way up the road on their route to the Health Food Stores. There were houses on both sides, some were quite expensive on the right. They had names that included the word villa.

They turned left opposite the cemetery; these houses were smaller and had names that included the word cottage.

They started to walk along the road, when Reggie stopped still. 'There's a funny smell,' he said.

'What smell?'

'Don't know,' said Reggie. He walked on, stood still and sniffed the air. 'I don't know what it is ... but it is not right. It reminds me of the smell, when Auntie Bee is clearing out the range.'

The children look around, and spotted black smoke coming out of a chimney of one of the cottages.

'I reckon that chimney is on fire,' shouted Reggie. 'FIRE, FIRE, FIRE. We need the fire brigade.'

Reggie went up to the front door of the house and banged the knocker, shouting all the time.

A man came out of the house next door and ran into the street. 'There is a lady in there, but she'll be in bed. She is a nurse and was on duty last night.'

'Do you have a phone,' asked Lindy. 'We need the fire brigade.'

'No, I don't but the shop will,' he replied.

'I'll go to the shop and get them to call,' said Lindy.

The man joined Reggie thumping on the door and shouting. There was no response.'

'She may be upstairs asleep,' said the man.

'Which room does she sleep in?' Reggie asked.

'I don't really know, but I often see her putting up the blackouts to the front bedroom.

Quick as a flash, Reggie jumped up grabbed the drain pipe and preceded to climb up the outside of the building to the window sill. Holding tight with his finger tips, he yelled, 'Wake up, Wake up! FIRE, FIRE.'

With the noise of the man hammering on the front door, Reggie banging on the window and the two shouting, the lady of the house appeared between the curtains. She lifted the sash window and Reggie jumped in.

'Your chimney is on fire. Have you got a stirrup pump?'

'Yes, it's on the landing,' she said running out of the door.

Reggie noticed a small hatch in the chimney breast. His hand went towards it.

'No! Don't touch it, it's HOT!' said the nurse. 'You need a cloth.'

'Reggie picked up the nearest piece of cloth he could lay his hands on. It was the nurses uniform dress. He quickly folded it so it was thicker and opened the cast iron hatch. He was greeted with a roar of a fire and thick smoke coming out.

The lady returned with a bucket full of water and a stirrup pump tucked under her arm. 'I always have a bucket ready, just in case,' she said.

'You pump,' said Reggie, 'and I'll direct the spray of water through this hatch. Hopefully this will hold the fire until the brigade comes.'

She pumped and Reggie held the hose in the hole. The nurse had a powerful pumping action, and the water ran out in no time.

'I'll get another bucket,' she said, 'It's on the landing.'

'We need to open the front door and let the fire brigade in,' said Reggie. 'You go and unlock the front door and I'll fill up the bucket again. Where's the nearest tap?'

'Downstairs in the kitchen! We have no bathroom, but the other bucket just outside this door is full. I'll take the empty one and refill it.'

With the empty bucket swinging on her arm the nurse ran downstairs and unlocked the front door. The man from next door was there.

'What can I do to help?' he offered.

'Fill up the bucket and bring it upstairs,' the nurse said. 'I'll go back and pump.' He filled it from the kitchen tap and carried it up to the nurse who was on the landing just outside the bedroom door. As soon as he had put it down, he took the empty one down to refill it. Reggie kept up the spray of water into the hatch.

Five buckets later, there was a shout from down stairs. 'Hello up there!' It was the fire brigade.

The nurse left the pumping, and directed the men to the front room where there was a fire in the hearth. The man from next door was in the kitchen filling up the bucket.

'My bedroom is directly above this room,' she said. 'And there is a young boy up there trying to put out the fire.' A fireman hurried upstairs just as Reggie was trying to work out how he could pump and hold the hose at the same time. He decided he'd put the hose in the hole leave it and start to pump again.

'Reggie! it's you!' said William. 'Leave this now, we are here to deal with this. Stop pumping as the water you are putting into the chimney will get hot and scald the men downstairs. You have done a marvellous job, well done.'

Reggie stood against the wall and watched. Two further firemen came upstairs.

'This is Reggie, he is my daughter's friend,' said William.

'Hello,' said Reggie. 'Lindy is outside waiting for me.'

'You go downstairs and join Lindy outside; we have everything under control.'

William was instructed to check the other bedroom, the ceilings, walls and the loft. 'You never know where the fire has spread to,' said one of the firemen, 'I'll check the houses each side of this one. Did you work the stirrup pump?'

'Yes sir, me and the lady. The man from next door filled the buckets.'

Reggie went downstairs but couldn't resist having a look at what the firemen were doing in the sitting room. He peered over the banisters and spotted a cone with small holes in it, which reminded him of a watering can. It was attached to a hose, also attached next to it was a bamboo cane. At the bottom of this was a brass screw. The fireman pushed the cane up the chimney and when it was at the point when the next push would have made it disappear, another fireman attached a further cane to the screw head.

'Is that tight enough Charley?' someone said. 'Yep, push away,' was the reply. They pushed the cane further up the chimney. At the same time two other firemen were working the pump and bucket. One was pumping the other was refilling another one. Their pump was much bigger than the one that had been used upstairs. A further bamboo cane was added and more water added to the bucket.

'You have done a good job!' said William. 'Well done, Reggie.'

'Yes, well done son,' said the fireman. 'I am Mr Brading the commander.'

With the fire out and drama over, Reggie flopped down on the floor at the foot of the stairs. He suddenly became aware of his surroundings, and of the contrast between the large men fully clothed in heavy dark serge uniforms, and a small woman in just a thin pair of silky pyjamas. He was suddenly reminded of Jane, the Daily Mirror cartoon. *I'm in the wrong place, I shouldn't be in here.* 'I'll be off now,' he called out as he tried to avert his eyes from the lady standing in front of him. He walked towards the front door.

'Thank you,' said the lady as she stood back to let him through.

'That's alright!' Reggie called back as he turned his head away not looking at her at all.

Outside the front door, there was a crowd of people, all wanting to see something connected with the incident. He found Lindy and took her hand firmly. With his head down he pushed his way through the crowd.

'It must have been a fire, because the fire brigade is here,' said one lady.

'It wasn't down to Hitler then, there was no air raid warning,' said another.

'Perhaps it was a delayed action bomb,' someone suggested.

'But there was no explosion,' an old gentleman said.

'Maybe it was a delayed action incendiary,' said another voice. 'Devious people these Germans.'

'Or one that hadn't gone off.'

Neither Lindy nor Reggie responded to the comments, their minds were on shopping and getting it done.

The mass of people at the house had created one good advantage, as there was no queue at the Health Food Stores. The crowd had left the shop to see what was happening up the road. In the shop Lindy and Reggie were able to be served immediately and finished their shopping in record time, however there were queues at the other shops. Once they had got all they needed they made their way to Cross Street and caught the bus home.

At the supper table that night, the conversation between Arthur, Lindy and Cludgy was all about the muddy washing. It wasn't until William joined them that the story of Reggie and the chimney fire was relayed.

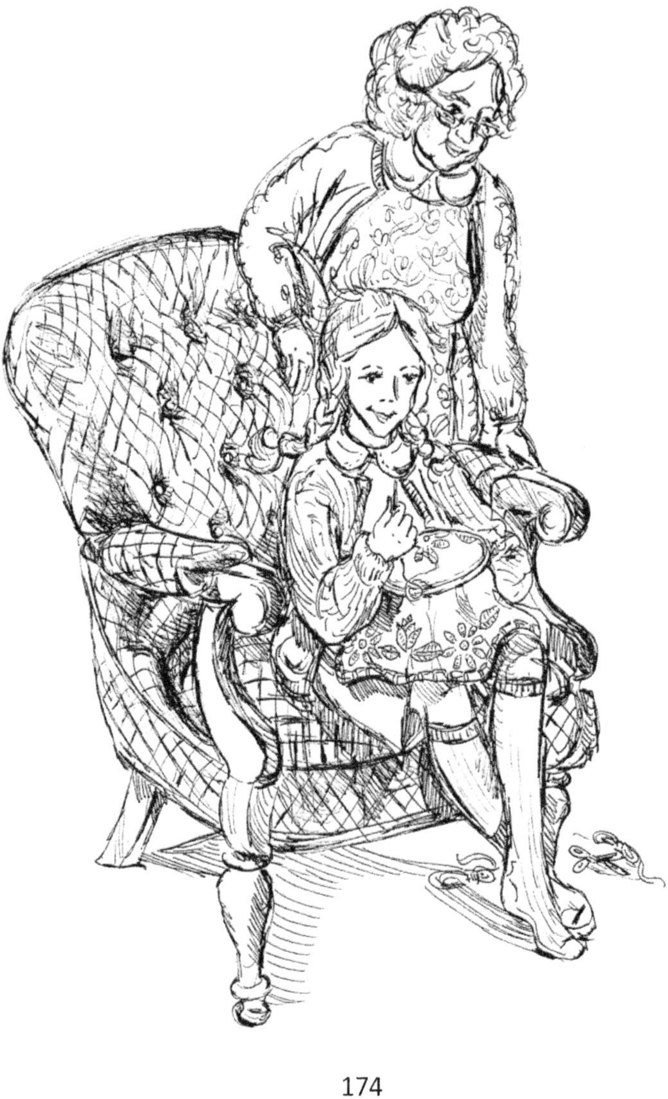

22
The Birthday

Since the Battle of Britain, the Island had been on high alert as planes flew over on their way to attack London, Southampton and other major cities on the mainland. To make their planes lighter, thus faster in their efforts to get away, many German pilots dropped their bombs on the island, some falling on Ryde. None had made a direct hit on the convent school, but upon close inspection it was discovered that the vibrations from these bombs had cause some damage to the building. It was decided that repairs needed to take place, and consequently the girls were given a day off school to give the workmen space to effect the repairs.

Since the incident with the maths homework, Clarissa and Lindy had been good friends. It was Clarissa's birthday on the 4th of May. The day chosen for these repairs was to be on the same day. Clarissa was beside herself with joy. She was to have a day off on her birthday.

'I'm afraid a party this year is out of the questions,' Clarissa's mother said. 'But would you like to have a friend over to our house? You could play all evening and perhaps she could stay the night.'

'Oh yes, that would be good, may I ask Lindy Elliot to come?'

'Have I met Lindy?'

'Probably not, she lives in Little Bridge and is an evacuee from Portsmouth.'

'An evacuee! From Portsmouth! Are you sure she is the right sort of girl to have as a friend.' Clarissa's mother was a little anxious. She had heard some bad stories about evacuees.

'What is she like?' she asked her daughter. 'Are you sure she is polite and well mannered?'

'Oh Mum of course she is. She used to go to a private school in Brighton before she was evacuated.'

'Well alright then. If you are sure,' her mother said. 'Invite her by all means.'

'My birthday is on the 4th. She could come on the Monday, stay the night and then we can go to school together the following day.'

The date was set. Clarissa gave Lindy a letter which was given to Cludgy, to make sure all was well with her. The letter was written on personally headed top quality writing paper. It was signed 'The Hon Mrs Louisa Fanny Robinson'.

'Oh, my goodness! She is an honourable,' said Cludgy.

'What does that mean?' said Lindy. 'Does it matter?'

'No, I don't think so, she is a mother of a friend of yours and I am your foster mother. It shouldn't matter at all.'

Cludgy wrote a reply. She made sure that her spelling was correct and her writing neat.

Once a reply was received and permission given, Clarissa's mother made plans.

I could use my meat ration sparingly and fill the plate up with as many fresh vegetables as I can lay my hands on. I'll hide the lack of meat with lots of gravy. She thought to herself. *I'll borrow a mattress from my neighbour. I have enough blankets; I was given so many as wedding presents when I got married.*

After lunch on Monday 4th May, Lindy's small brown suitcase was packed. Cludgy made sure that she had her night clothes which were washed and ironed before packing. Her wash bag contained her tooth brush, her flannel and in a little box, a tiny piece of soap. She also packed a small towel.

Cludgy was still a little concerned and suddenly aware of her status in society. Clarissa's mother was the daughter of an 'honourable' who had gained his title working in the Diplomatic Service in the Far East. Clarissa's father also had worked at the same place but in a much lower role. He was a clerk. The Robinson family had returned to England in 1939 just before war was declared. Her father was just an ordinary man, however her mother liked to live up to her perceived station in life.

'I suggest you wear your school uniform,' said Cludgy, 'then you will be ready to go to school the next day. Make sure you wash before going to bed. Hang your uniform neatly over a chair, so it is smart for the next day.'

'I will!' said Lindy

'And don't forget to clean your teeth.'

'I will …' said Lindy. 'I mean I won't … forget.'

'Best behaviour too! Don't forget your 'P's' and 'Q's'.

'I will, I mean I won't,' said Lindy. 'I'll catch the number four bus which arrives at the bottom of the hill at ten past two. Clarissa said she would meet me when I got to the bus stop at the recreation ground in East Cowes.'

Carrying her school bag, her lunch box, gas mask and overnight suitcase, Lindy was laden. She hadn't reached the church gate before Reggie came bounding up behind her. 'Shall I carry your suitcase for you Lindy?'

'Oh, Reggie you are a star! Yes please.'

'You look like a pack horse!'

'Thanks, I'm not sure that being compared with a horse is a compliment.'

'Where are you going?'

'I'm spending the night with Clarissa in East Cowes. It's her birthday. She lives near the recreation ground on the main road. What are you doing today?'

'I am going to the fire station for some training. It's for my fireman's badge.'

'On a Monday?' asked Lindy.

'Yes, they were busy last Thursday and so the training had to be changed.'

'How are you getting on with all your badges?'

'Oh, very well, I think I am the best one there!'

'Really!' said Lindy thinking, *Reggie is never short of bravado!*

She was grateful for Reggie's help. Despite having very little in the bag, it was rather heavy. They crossed the road and Reggie put it down. 'I'll wait with you until the bus arrives,' said Reggie. 'Then I can pass your case to the conductor.'

'Thanks Reggie, you are a gentleman.'

'Well, it is the right thing to do, isn't it?' he turned away feeling a little embarrassed.

When the bus arrived, the conductor was nowhere to be seen. Reggie got on the bus and put her bag in the space under the stairs which was set aside for luggage. Lindy climbed on and found a seat.

'Hold very tight please,' shouted the conductor from upstairs. He pressed the bell twice.

'Hang on!' shouted Reggie as he quickly turned around and jumped off the moving bus. Lindy waved to Reggie and mouthed, 'Thank you.'

'I didn't even have time to say goodbye,' said Reggie to himself. 'What an impatient conductor!'

Lindy was used to travelling on her own, she had travelled from Portsmouth to her school in Brighton many times. She put her lunch box on the seat at the side of her, her school bag on her lap, and then sat back to enjoy the journey. It was a fine day, making the views out of the window more pleasing. The Mill Pond at Wootton looked lovely and Lindy was sure she saw what she thought to be a

Heron bird flying off. She made a mental note to remember that and look it up when she got home tomorrow.

The conductor approached her, she took her money out of her bag on her lap.

'Going to school?' quipped the conductor.

'No, I am going to East Cowes to see my friend. It is her birthday.'

'Nice, hope you have a good time,' he said as he turned the handle on his ticket machine.

As she put her purse back into her bag, she noticed the birthday present parcel for Clarissa. With Cludgy's help she had embroidered a dressing table cloth. *I hope it's alright and she likes it, I had a bit of trouble with the last leaf.* It was done using satin stitch, which she had found a little difficult. For a birthday card, she found a picture of some flowers in an old magazine in Cludgy's loft. She cut them out and stuck them onto a piece of stiff paper, folded it and wrote a birthday message inside.

Closing her bag firmly she settled back for the last part of the journey.

At the bottom of Lushington Hill, she was struck by two cottages side by side in the middle of nowhere except the road. *What bleak and isolated houses. They would make a good subject for a story.*

Clarissa was waiting for Lindy at the bus stop in East Cowes.

'Happy Birthday Clarissa!' called Lindy.

'Hello Lindy,' said Clarissa who was waiting with her mother. 'Let me help you with your things.'

'Thank you. They are a bit cumbersome,' said Lindy. Reggie helped me to the bus stop at Little Bridge.'

'May I introduce you to my mother,' said Clarissa. 'Mother this is Lindy.

'How do you do?' said Lindy politely as she put down her bag and put out her hand.

Clarissa's mother shook Lindy's hand and said, 'How do you do?'

They walked together across the recreation field, to their house.

'Clarissa, show Lindy your room and where she is to sleep tonight.' They thundered upstairs and went into her bedroom where another bed had been set up.

Lindy gave Clarissa the card and parcel containing the embroidered dressing table cloth. She opened the card first as according to her mother was the right thing to do.

'What a lovely card! Thank you.' She stood it up on her chest of drawers.

Then she picked up the parcel. At first, she undid the string and then slowly opened the paper. Inside was a freshly ironed and beautifully folded embroidered cloth.

'Oh, this is lovely!' said Clarissa taking it out of the paper. 'I shall treasure it.'

As the cloth lay on Clarrisa's bed, Lindy noticed the leaf that had caused her so much difficulty was now very neat. *I suspect that Cludgy unpicked it and sewed it again.* She thought to herself.

Lindy opened her case and laid her nightdress out ready for the night. She took out her toilet bag and put that on the chair by the bed.

Clarissa removed her hair brush and mirror from the dressing table and laid out her new dressing table cloth that Lindy had given her.

'There, that looks lovely. Thank you once again.'

The girls went downstairs and into the kitchen. Standing in the middle of the room was a large table with strong steel bars around three sides. Inside was a bed, made up and ready to use.

'This is a Morrison shelter, but we also made another shelter under the stairs,' said Clarissa's mother. 'I think it would be a good idea if you two would use that one.'

'We had a raid on the 28th of last month,' said Clarissa, 'so I'm hoping that we don't have one tonight.'

The two girls practised climbing into the reinforced space under the stairs.

They went back into the kitchen; the Morrison shelter was now a table. It was laid and on it was a lovely supper of fresh vegetables, meat and gravy. Lindy was not sure what the meat was, but thought it best not to ask.

It was strange eating from their table as it was quite high off the ground and the chairs were too low for it. Two pillows had been put on their chairs to make them higher, however it was only their head and shoulders that were visible. Their knees were pressing on the steel bars.

'Now what would you like to call me?' asked Clarissa's Mum. 'How about Auntie Muriel?'

'Thank you, Auntie Muriel,' said Lindy. 'And thank you for this lovely meal.'

'Oh, but there is more!' said Auntie Muriel, she left the table and went into the scullery. After a short while she returned with a small cake on a large long platter, also on the plate was a large candle. 'There now Clarissa, blow out your pretend birthday candle.'

23
Training for the Fireman's Badge

After the chimney fire, Reggie's confidence was sky high. He had dealt with an incident, a chimney fire. He had recognised it as an emergency, long before anyone else. He had kept his cool, and dealt with it in an efficient way. This was the second time he had dealt with a fire. In November, 1940 with the aid of his father he had put out a fire in the church.

Soon after the chimney incident William had praised him for 'his quick thinking,' and even Mr Brading, the Station Officer at the Edward Street sub-station, said how well he had done. So, on his way to the fire station for training, he thought there would be more praise and recognition of his action. As he marched smartly into the appliance bay of the fire station, he expected someone to say something about the chimney fire.

'Evening Reggie,' said Mr Brading. 'Ready for training? I shall be taking it today.'

'Evening sir,' he replied. Much to Reggie's anguish, he said nothing about the chimney fire.

He bumped into Ronald, a fellow scout but two years older. 'Hello Reggie,' said Ronald, 'you are going to enjoy tonight's training.'

'Am I?' said Reggie.

Tom, a new member of the scout troop wanting to do the fireman's badge walked in.

'Hello Tom,' shouted Reggie.

'Hello Reggie,' said Tom nervously. 'It's my first time here, where do we go?'

'We wait here to be told,' answered Reggie. He so wanted to talk about his chimney fire, but to mention it would be showing off, and he would get laughed at. He thought it better not to say anything.

Three more scouts arrived. First was Henry who was in the Home Guard then David and Malcolm, first aiders who worked with the red cross nurse Peggy Vaughan.

'Follow me,' said Mr Brading. 'We are going up to the Recreation Room.'

The boys walked smartly up the stairs, except for Tom who was in awe of where he was. He was slight in stature and all the vehicles looked so enormous.

'Buck up Tom!' called Henry, 'we want to get there today not tomorrow!'

'Alright! I'm coming.' Tom fastened his pace and ran up the last few steps. When he arrived, he was faced with tables and chairs. He spotted on one wall a darts board with chalkboards either side ready for the next game. He stood and looked around and he spotted in one corner a shiny pole. His eyes were fixed on this which was about four inches thick. Following the pole down he discovered that there was a large hole in the floor. The pole went straight through to where he had stood and looked at the fire trucks. He couldn't work it out. *Why would they leave a hole in the floor?* he thought.

'Tom!' called Mr Brading. 'Over here lad, we are about to start.'

Tom stood still staring at the hole. He wanted to ask what it was and why it was there? But nothing came out, he was left just pointing at the pole and the hole with his mouth open.

'You'll have a go at that when you have finished learning what I am about to teach you. Come on over and sit down.'

The boys gathered around the black board.

'There was a Red Warning earlier today,' said Mr. Brading, 'But it has been a quiet day and a fine one so we have decided to carry on with the training. However, if the alarm goes off ... you know the drill. I disappear and you all disperse to your homes.' He turned to the blackboard. 'Today I am going to talk about the triangle of fire; in other words, the three elements that make up a fire.' He turned to the board, picked up his chalk and put it on the board ready to write.

'Oh bother,' moaned Ronald. 'I think we are in for a theory lesson.'

As Mr Brading wrote on the board, he said each word. 'The ... Triangle ... of ... fire.'

Just as he was writing the last word, Reggie said in a loud whisper, 'Sounds like a title for a good film!' The boys sniggered.

'Yes, it does Reggie. I know that was you! I have eyes in the back of my head. Perhaps you would be so kind as to do all the rest of the writing, then I won't have to turn my back to the class.'

Reggie was a little nervous of writing words on the board, although his writing had improved, his spelling still needed a lot of work.

'Yes sir. It would be a pleasure.' Reggie knew he was bluffing; he would much rather sit and not possibly be made a fool of by his poor spelling.

'The triangle of fire,' Mr Brading repeated. Reggie drew a perfectly formed triangle.

Mr Brading turned around and looked at the blackboard. 'My! my!' he said, 'if my eyes don't deceive me, that is a perfectly drawn equilateral triangle.'

'Thank you, sir,' said Reggie not knowing what an equilateral triangle was. He didn't let on he didn't know.

'The three elements are heat as in a flame'; Reggie drew a flame at the top of the triangle. 'Thank you, that's perfect. Next is fuel. Now what burns easily. This is where you all can help me. I'll start and say, paper ...' he stopped talking as Reggie had already drawn a piece of paper. It was scrunched up like into a loose ball. 'Auntie Bee makes these when she is lighting a fire.' Reggie informed the group.

'Chairs!' shouted Ronald. 'They are made of wood, they'll burn.' Reggie drew a chair.

'Sofas' shouted David. A sofa was added to the board.

'Dry sticks,' said Malcolm.

'That's easy to draw,' said Reggie.

'A table!' shouted David. Reggie had just drawn the fourth leg of the table when Malcolm shouted 'A table cloth.' Reggie added a cloth to the table.

'Curtains!'

'Cushions!'

'Clothes! said Tom. 'You know when they are on the clothes horse, drying by the fire.'

'Alright lads! I think we shall stop there. We have got the idea.' Reggie finished by drawing a pair of trousers hanging on a clothes horse.

'Now can anyone think of what should be added to the remaining angle of the triangle?'

There was silence. Reggie remembered how Auntie Bee blows on the base of the fire when she is getting the range to light.

'Blowing! Is it air sir?'

'Would you like to explain Reggie?'

'When you light a fire, you blow at the bottom and the flames rise up.'

'You are right, but the word I am looking for is Oxygen. Later when we have finished our talk, we will go downstairs into the yard outside and you can see this in practice. We will light a fire and then we will put it out. Now we must not delay, as we can't light fires after the sun goes down and the blackouts are put up.'

'No sir,' said Malcolm. 'You'll have Mr Curtess our ARP warden after you.'

'Or Peter, he's in the ARP.'

'I would be after you!' said Peter, as he pointed to his armband stating "ARP." 'It's against the law.'

'But more importantly,' continued Mr Brading. 'A fire is easily seen from the sky; we don't want the Germans to see us.'

Mr Brading continued his talk, explaining the need to shut all doors, if possible, to cut out the drafts and reduce the oxygen which is keeping the fire alight. And if the fire was out, a draft could reignite any embers that may still be alight.

'Please sir, what if the Germans had bombed and the door wasn't there,' said David. Mr Brading ignored him.

'Shut up David,' said Malcolm. 'If there wasn't a door, then you couldn't shut it, could you?'

Mr Brading went to the back of the room and came back carrying a bucket and a stirrup pump.

'Right now,' said Mr Brading raising his voice to regain control of his class, 'Before we go down stairs, I must explain what a stirrup pump is and more importantly how it works.'

'He put the bucket on the floor. The hose he gave to Ronald to direct to an imaginary fire under the darts board.

'The pump goes in the bucket full of water,' said Mr Brading. 'Now I need a volunteer to pump.' Everyone's hands went up. 'Henry, would you like to pretend to pump for me.'

'Can't we have real water sir?' said Tom.

'Not up here. We will have water when we go downstairs. Now with Henry pumping efficiently, so that Ronald can direct the water on to the fire, the bucket will soon empty.' He stopped speaking and turned around. 'Oh bother,' he said to himself. 'I have forgotten to get another bucket.'

No-one had seen Reggie leave the room. He had remembered how the nurse had to replenish the bucket. So, he had run into the kitchen and taken the enamel washing up bowl out of the sink and brought it back.

'Here you are sir,' he said, pretending to carry the bowl as if heavy and full of water. He thought he might pretend to drop it all over Mr Brading, but decided that was a step too far.

'Thank you, Reggie. Can you add the imaginary water to the bucket please.'

The boys took turns to pump, to direct the hose at the fire and replenish the bucket.

'Now the real thing!' said Mr Brading. 'Let's go downstairs to the yard.'

24
Real Fire and Real Water

'Can we use the pole?' said Reggie.

'Yes. That is the plan,' said Mr Brading. 'Do you want to go first?'

The boys stood up, scraping their chairs in unison, and rushed over to the hole.

'Boys! You have left the chairs all over the place, please return to them and push them in.' Equally quickly the boys did as they were told, rushed to their seats, and scraped the floor again as they pushed them under the tables. Then speedily they returned to the line, all except Tom. He still didn't understand what the pole was for, and why there was a hole.

Tom slowly walked to the back of the queue. Just as Reggie launched himself onto the pole and slid down.

'Wheeeee!' he shouted as he went.

The others followed one by one. Reggie was upstairs again in time to watch Henry the last but one boy, to have his go. Tom stood back.

'Can I have another go?' said Reggie.

'Slow down, it's Tom's turn,' said Mr Brading. 'Wait a minute. Tom, don't you want to do it?'

'Yes, but I don't know how to. Why do you need a pole?'

'Because it's quicker to get down to the Appliance Bay. When there's an emergency, we need to be quick. Very quick.'

'Oh! I suppose that's right,' said Tom.

'Let's go through this slowly.' They stood looking at the pole and the hole.

'Now Tom, the first thing you do is put your left hand on the pole in line with your head, then you put your right hand just below it.' Mr Brading was demonstrating by holding an imaginary pole in front of him. 'Then you wrap your left foot around the pole and add your right foot. Your feet make a sandwich of the pole. Your two feet squeeze together thus making them act like a brake. Obviously, I can't demonstrate that bit, because I will fall over. He laughed. Tom didn't. His face remained serious and focused on Mr Brading. At the bottom there is a mat about four inches thick to cushion your landing.'

'Shall I do it again to show him,' said Reggie.

'Yes, a good idea, but can you do each action really slowly.'

'Yes sir, shall I start now?'

'Yes please.'

Reggie never does things by halves. He walked extremely slowly across to the hole. Equally at the same speed, his left hand moved through the air to the pole, his right hand did the same. 'Slow enough Sir?' he said. Then he put his left leg on the pole, and his right leg joined it.

Squeezing his feet together tightly, he remained in the same position. 'Shall I go down now?'

Mr Brading was laughing. 'You look like a monkey,' he said. Tom couldn't see the joke. Reggie released the squeeze between his feet and like a monkey shot down the pole as quick as a flash. At the bottom, Reggie released his hold, stood to attention and bowed.

'Ever the clown,' said Mr Brading.

'I'll wait at the bottom sir, for Tom to arrive,' said Reggie 'and catch him if I need to.'

Slowly and steadily, Tom first put his hands around the pole, then added one leg and then, when his other leg had left the floor above and grasped the pole, he slid down to the floor below.'

'Cor! That was good,' said Tom. 'Can I do it again?' Reggie moved him out of the way just in time to avoid Mr Brading as he slid down the pole and landed next to the boys.

'No, you can't we have too much to do before blackout. Another time, when we are not so busy.'

Outside in the yard there were two metal trays with high sides. Next to them were newspapers, sticks and a box of matches.

'So, THIS is the fun bit,' said Reggie.

'Quiet everyone, we don't have a lot of time left,' said Mr Brading. 'The sun sets at 9.29, and at that point we must have the blackouts up and our fires must be extinguished.'

'Are we lighting fires?' asked Tom. 'I've never been allowed to do that.'

'I know how to light a fire please sir,' said Reggie. 'Please may I do it?'

'I know you always like to volunteer, but I'll ask one of the others. Peter, would you like to light the fire?'

'Yes sir!' He stepped forward. 'I've not done this before and I'm not really sure.'

'I'll talk you through it,' said Mr Brading.

Under Mr Brading's instruction, Peter loosely scrunched up some newspaper and laid it in the tray, then he added some dry twigs like a wigwam.

'This shape allows a lot of air to get in,' said Mr Brading. 'And a fire needs ... what? ... can someone tell me please?'

'Oxygen!' shouted Tom.

'Well done, Tom,' said Mr Brading.

Peter took the box of matches, and lit one. He moved towards the fire, but by the time he had got there the match had gone out.

'You need to start closer to the fire.' Peter knelt down and held the match box closer.'

'No, you need to be closer than that,' said Mr Brading.

'Won't I get burnt?'

'No, there is no explosive in it. Only paper and twigs, the flame from the match will take a few seconds to catch the paper alight.'

Mr Brading got on his knees next to Peter and guided his hands closer to the fire. Peter struck the match and held it close to the paper. After a few seconds it lit.

'Move back now, but keep an eye on it, we don't want it to go out.'

Mr Brading turned away from the fire to speak to the group. 'Do you understand the triangle we spoke about upstairs?'

Reggie suddenly spotted the fire going out. The paper had almost finished burning and the twigs had not yet caught alight. He dropped to his knees next to the fire, and blew into the base of it. With steady breaths he encouraged the flames to rise catching the twigs alight until there was a steady fire burning.

'Thank you, Reggie,' said Mr Brading. He looked at the sky, and looked at his watch. 'Now we must hurry it is nearly black out time. The next job is to put the fire out. I've arranged for one more fire so that you can all have a go using the stirrup pump.'

'Please sir, I've used a stirrup pump twice now, shall I light the other fire for you,' said Reggie.

'Thanks that would be most helpful,' he replied. 'I'll leave you to it.'

'If you remember,' said Reggie. 'I helped put out the chimney fire … in …' Reggie's voice drifted away and he stopped speaking as no one was listening. The group were concentrating on Mr Brading and the stirrup pumps.

I'll show 'em, Reggie thought. He scrunched up a whole copy of the Daily Mirror, after having read the antics of the Jane cartoon. He found the thinnest and driest twigs he could and placed them over the large amount of paper balls. He took two matches, placed the end of one in his mouth to hold. He lay down close to the fire, and was about to strike the match when he thought he had better tell Mr Brading. He took out the spare match from his mouth and shouted, 'Shall I light the fire sir?'

'Yes please,' called Mr Brading. 'When you are ready.'

He put the spare match back in his mouth, struck and lit the first one. It caught a newspaper ball; he put the tiny flame to a second ball and then a third. Finally, he struck the spare match that had been in his mouth and lit the last few. It took a few seconds and then up went the flames where the fire had caught the newspaper. Carefully and slowly, he added the twigs. Until a quite substantial fire was burning in the tin tray in the yard.

'My goodness!' said Mr Brading, 'I'm not sure whether we should put that fire out as part of the lesson, or sing camp fire songs around it.'

The group stood around it admiring the flames.

'It seems a shame we have to extinguish it,' said Mr Brading. 'But put it out, we have too. I think we could use both stirrup pumps to tackle that one. Now organise yourselves. All the members of the team have a responsible job when working the stirrup pump. You can't put a fire out without someone holding the hose in the right place. You can't put the fire out unless someone is pumping the water through, and you can't pump the water out unless there is enough in the bucket. Right lads off you go. Two groups of three. Direct the water onto the base of the fire. Well done!'

Reggie was quite happy to be the bucket filler, as he ran backwards and forwards from the tap to fill them. The fires out, the yard was cleared in the dim light and the blackouts were put up.

'Well done lads,' Mr. Brading said. 'You have worked well tonight, now hurry home whilst there is still some light. See you all next week unless something unexpected happens. Good night.'

'Thank you, sir,' said the boys in return.

25
Not Another Red Sky

It was a quarter to ten when the boys finally left. They had all been allowed a further turn on the pole. They slid down and ran up the stairs to repeat it, again and again until Mr Brading told them to stop. Tom enjoyed it the most, he had learnt a new skill and he wanted to practise it as much as possible.

Reggie lingered in the Appliance Bay looking at the selection of vehicles.

'They are all named,' said Reggie's friend Colin, one of the firemen.

'What?' said Reggie. 'You give them names?'

'Let me introduce you to Ethel,' said the fireman.

'Ethel! Why Ethel?' said Reggie.

'It is the name of the wife of the Mayor of Ryde.'

'Doesn't she mind her name being used for a fire lorry? I mean it's not very ... very ...'

'Glamourous?' said Colin. 'No, she was very flattered. I know that for a fact as she is my mother.'

'Oh,' said Reggie who couldn't think of anything to say.

'When we ride on the back of that, we have to hang on for our lives, especially if Browney is driving, as he can get quite a speed out of her. We are used to it now.'

They walked around the vehicle; Reggie climbed onto it and wondered what bit he would hang on to if he were a fireman going to an emergency.

'At our other fire station in Edward Street,' Colin said, 'there is a fire engine called Alice. I don't know who she was. There is a trailer pump which is towed by an old Post box van, and of course there is Mr Brading's coal lorry. They were both fitted with a tow bar after they were donated to the war effort.'

'You have got a lot of lorries. I would love to drive one of those.'

'You are a bit too young at the moment. One day perhaps...'

'They all look very smart, I bet they are valuable,' said Reggie.

'Yes, you are right there, they are all very valuable whatever their age or condition, extremely valuable to the war effort and not easily replaced.'

Reggie looked at the hoses and pointed to something bright and shining.

'That is called a coupling. There is a freshwater well at Edward Street, and we use it to wash out the hoses and pumps as they have been pumping sea water full of salt. One day we dropped one of these couplings into the well by accident. We knew we couldn't replace it, so we pumped out the well and using a ladder sent one of the lads down it to retrieve it. The trouble was that the water kept refilling the well so he only had a little time to recover it.'

Reggie was fascinated. 'But it all turned out well in the end, didn't it? I mean they got the bit and he didn't drown!'

'No, he didn't drown! His uniform did get very wet though!' They laughed.

'I don't see your friend Bill here.'

'No, he had to leave the fire service as he was needed to be a fire watcher on the top of Ryde Town Hall.'

'Shame, he was good fun,' said Reggie. 'Especially when he helped with the training.'

'I've an idea, he gets very bored and cold up there, why don't you nip to the town hall and visit him. There's a door at the back that will be open. Once in there you will see the stairs that go up.'

Reggie knew it was late and that he should go home, but the temptation of climbing up to the top of Ryde Town Hall was too great. *I won't take long,* he convinced himself, *I can get back quickly along Spencer Road and Ladies Lane and be home in no time.*

Reggie found the door and opened it silently. *Why am I being quiet, nobody's here except Bill on the roof.* He ascended endless flights of steps but eventually he reached a narrow set of stairs. He climbed them and opened the door at the top. In front of him was Bill dressed in a warm duffle coat and woolly hat.

'Hello Bill!' Reggie called.

'Hello, I can't see you, who are you?'

'Reggie Mitchell. Don't you remember me? We have met already, at the cinema. I'm a friend of Colin's. I have just been doing some training at the fire station. He said perhaps you would like a visitor.'

'Oh yes, I remember. Hello Reggie. A visitor? How nice. It does get a bit lonely up here at night.'

Bill put his binoculars up to his eyes and looked around. 'All quiet at the moment,' he said.

Bill and Reggie gazed across the Solent. 'How odd it still seemed that even on a clear night not a speck of light could be seen coming from the south coast.'

'May I see through your binoculars?'

'I'm not supposed to ... but just for a minute then.' He took them off over his head and handed them to Reggie.

'Put the strap over your head, they mustn't be dropped as they may break.'

Bill turned him around and explained in which direction was Portsmouth and Southampton. 'Can't see anything can you?' said Bill. 'That's because the blackout works! Everyone has their blackouts up.'

'My mum is in Southampton, building bits for Spitfires.'

'Should you be telling me that? Careless talks costs lives, so the poster says.'

Bill opened his satchel which had been lying on the floor. He took out his tin sandwich box and a thermos.

'My mum makes far too many sandwiches for me would you like one? I think she has put Marmite in them tonight.'

'Yes please, if you can spare one,' said Reggie.

I've tea in the thermos but only one cup, I'm afraid,' said Bill. 'We'll have to share; I'll drink out of one side of the cup and you drink out of the other.'

'Gosh thanks very much.'

During their impromptu meal Reggie related how he had helped put out a chimney fire.

'Yes, I know, I heard about that from William Elliot. Well done!' said Bill. 'You should be proud of yourself.'

Reggie didn't know how to answer that. He was pleased with himself, but to say so would be showing off. So, he said nothing.

They sat quietly looking out into the inky blackness when Bill said, 'It's quite late shouldn't you be making your way home. Old Ted Rollings is joining me shortly.'

'Hmm I suppose so,' said Reggie. 'It's much more fun with you up here.'

'Don't tell anyone you were on the roof of the town hall with me, or I will get into trouble.'

'No, I won't. Promise.'

Bill took his binoculars from Reggie and put them up to his eyes again and did another sweep of the area around. He pointed them in the direction of blacked out Portsmouth and Southampton and saw nothing. But as he continued to sweep around, he was aware of a red sky over the north of the island. 'That's Cowes!' he said. 'And if I'm not mistaken flares are being dropped.'

He gave the binoculars to Reggie and he looked towards the area to the north.

'I think you are right!' said Reggie. As he handed the glasses back, there was a rumble and the roof beneath them seemed to shake.

'And that was heavy explosives being dropped. You must get home. I think Cowes is under attack.'

'Cowes! Lindy's in East Cowes,' said Reggie. 'I must get over there.'

'Don't be daft!' said Bill. 'East Cowes is miles away, how are you going to get there.'

'I'll borrow Lindy's bike it's at home in Little Bridge. I can cycle really quickly. I'll be there in no time.'

'Think about this Reggie,' said Bill. 'It's too far away and when you get there, how are you going to find her.'

'I know roughly where she is staying. She told me earlier.'

'Reggie don't be daft, you'll never find her. Think again!'

His wise words were lost as Reggie ran across the roof and back down the stairs.

Once in the street below, he ran along Spencer Road, and then Ladies Lane, planning as he ran what he would do when he got there. *I'll tell Auntie Bee that as a messenger I have an important document to deliver. She'll believe me, I must get to East Cowes.* At the cottages he found Lindy's bike easily in the shed in the walled garden. Auntie Bee came out of her front door.

'Reggie is that you?' she called.

'Yes, it's me,' said Reggie

'I'm a messenger this evening and I have an important document to deliver. I'll see you later. Shouldn't be too long.'

Not listening for her reply, he cycled off up the road. He took a short cut, through the woods, and along Quarry Road.

The night was clear, the stars and moon shone brightly enough for Reggie to see the road. His mind was focused on Lindy and getting to her.

As he approached East Cowes, the sound of the explosions and gun fire greeted him. He discovered the road was covered in bricks, glass and other debris. Unexpectedly an explosion knocked him off his bike. He decided to leave it in the hedge. I'll pick it up later. It'll be easy to remember where I left it as it is opposite the large imposing gates to Osborne House.'

Lindy had told him that Clarissa lived near the recreation field on the main road. *I'll make my way there.*

26
The Raid

The girls were sound asleep when the siren wailed. Lindy jumped out of bed and reached for her clothes. She couldn't find them! *Where are they?* she thought as she walked around the room.

'Lindy, are you alright?' said Clarissa.

She suddenly remembered where she was, and laid her hands on her clothes. 'Clarissa, we must get to the shelter.'

Lindy pushed her feet into her shoes as she pulled on her jumper at the same time. Grabbing her skirt, she followed Clarissa to the stairs.

They were half way down when there was an enormous bang. The front door was blown in and the girls were pushed back onto the stairs where they sat. Auntie Muriel was also blown backwards and was sitting on the floor in the hall. The bannisters were shattered and the door to the shelter under the stairs had come away from its hinges.

'That will give us no shelter now. Quickly girls; stay together.' Auntie Muriel pushed the kitchen door and realised that the side wall had been blown in and there were bricks, dust and glass all over the place. The way to the Morrison shelter was blocked, because the kitchen was full of debris.

'Right, we have lost both of our shelters, we will have to go to the communal shelter down the road. We'll go through what is left of the front entrance. Are you ready?'

'Yes,' they both said. Lindy had managed to get her skirt on but had not done it up, so holding her skirt up with one hand, she made her way over the glass and broken front door after Auntie Muriel and Clarissa.

Suddenly there was a whistling sound. 'Quickly,' shouted Auntie Muriel, 'Get down!' There was another loud explosion. Lying together they waited awhile, until some of the dust had settled. 'Come on you two,' Auntie Muriel shouted. 'We must get to a shelter.'

The three started to run, when without any warning there was another whistling sound and another explosion. Lindy lay down on the ground. She again waited for a few seconds, and then screamed.

'Clarissa! Clarissa! That was close, where are you?' she said. There was no reply. Getting up she looked around. Then she started to run but Clarissa and her mother had disappeared.

Lindy stood still and called out again. 'Clarissa! Clarissa! Auntie Muriel, oh where are you?'

She called and called them, but they were nowhere to be seen. There was so much noise that her voice was not heard. Standing alone, Lindy tried to listen for Clarissa's voice, calling her. She heard her name shouted, but it was not Clarissa.

'Lindy, Lindy! It's me Reggie. I heard your voice, where are you?'

The air was so thick with smoke and dust she could barely see a yard in front of her, seeing anyone or anything was difficult. She twisted, turned and looked left and right, up and down.

'Keep shouting my name,' said Reggie, 'stand still and I'll walk towards your voice.'

Lindy stood still terrified and shouted, 'Reggie, Reggie!'

'I'm coming to find you!' he said. 'Stay where you are and keep shouting my name.'

The smoke seemed to part, Lindy strained her eyes to see, then coming out of the gloom Reggie appeared and she was able to see her friend. The relief she felt was apparent in her voice. 'Oh Reggie, I am so glad to see you.'

'Me too.' said Reggie.

There was so much noise, as well as the roar made by the houses on fire, there were explosions and the "bof bof bof" from the guns firing on the invading planes. The whole scene was terrifying.

'Oh Reggie, I'm so glad I have found you. I am scared.'

'I'm scared too,' said Reggie.

She buried her face into Reggie shoulder, tears started to fall. 'What are you doing here?'

'I was on the roof of the town hall in Ryde with Bill and we witnessed the red sky over Cowes. We felt the vibration of the big bombs as they fell. I knew you were here so I came to find you. I thought you were with your friend, Clarissa! Where is she? And why aren't you in an air raid shelter?'

'I was with her, we had to leave the house as it was badly damaged. We were going to the shelter at the bottom of her road, when suddenly there was a large explosion and everyone ran. I was running too. We got separated and I can't find her.'

'You've found me,' said Reggie. 'I'm here with you. We are together now.'

Lindy clung on tight to Reggie's hand. 'We will face this together,' he said.

'We need to get out of here!' said Lindy.

There were fires all around, and mounds of bricks from broken houses everywhere. Visibility was difficult. The noise was excruciating, hearing each other's voices was very nearly impossible.

'Don't let go of my hand, will you Reggie?' Lindy shouted. He didn't hear. She looked at Reggie's face and repeated it as if she were talking to a deaf person.

'No of course not.' He replied using the same method, and then he paused. 'Lindy, don't you let go of my hand either.' Together they felt safer.

There were still people running to the shelters. Hand in hand they followed the group. In front of them there was an old lady being helped along by a young girl. The old lady's arm was over the little girl's shoulders. In front of them lay scattered bricks. The old lady stumbled on one and fell over taking the young girl with her.

'Nan!' the young girl called out. 'You must get up! We have got to get to the shelter.'

Lindy and Reggie rushed forward simultaneously letting go of each other's hands. One each side of the old lady, they put her arms over their shoulders and continued to the shelter.

'My bag!' shouted the old lady. 'My ration books are in there!'

'I've got them Nan don't worry,' said her granddaughter.

Supporting the old lady, they hurried together towards the brick-built air raid shelter. The roof of the shelter was flat; there were no windows; there was just a door at one end.

As they entered someone waved from the other end and shouted, 'Here Dot! Over here; I saved a space for you! Mary, sit on my lap and let your neighbour sit down.'

With the children's help the old lady squeezed through to her friend at the end.

'My granddaughter! Where is she?' Reggie found her and helped her through the crush of people.'

Lindy and Reggie sat on the floor holding hands. They said nothing, they just listened to bangs, crashes and the "bof bof bof" of the guns. Inside the shelter there was crying, someone was singing a hymn and another was praying. Lindy recognised a female voice saying, 'Hail Mary, full of grace ...' Lindy joined in.

Reggie looked at her, and when they had finished, he mouthed, 'What was that?'

'I know it from school. We say it before every lesson.'

It was very difficult not to be scared. Reggie knew he had to be calm, Lindy felt safer holding Reggie's hand, but the children were not prepared for the bomb that fell nearby. The ground shuddered violently, Lindy and Reggie clung together. The whole shelter seemed to be lifted up as the floor shook. The building settled and for a split second, there was silence. They were in darkness. 'I can't see!' someone shouted. 'Hang on I'll light my torch,' came a reply.

'We are trapped in! Oh, my saints!' said a voice from the other end of the building. 'Hail Mary, oh Hail Mary...' There was panic in her voice. The man standing at the door, shouted, 'The shelter next door has moved and is blocking our exit. '

'Oh God! Help us!' cries and screams were heard throughout the cramped structure.

Reggie remembered something that he had heard in one of his trainings. 'Hang on; we are not trapped.' He let go of Lindy's hand and climbed over bodies on the floor and reached the back wall.

'There are loose bricks here, I can smash a hole,' he said. There was shouting and so much noise from the guns and bombs outside, that no-one heard.

Reggie took off one of his sturdy boots; he put it over his hand. Then with the greatest force he could muster, he smashed the boot against the back wall. Two bricks moved and with a second strong hit they fell outside to the ground. The light from the fires streamed into the shelter. 'Here Lindy, hold my boot,' he called. 'I don't want to lose that.'

His two hands were now free, he pushed and pulled the bricks out, and created an exit. The shouting and crying subsided in the shelter as the occupants realised that there was a way out. On the other side of the wall that he had just broken, there were A.R.P. wardens and Firemen, also pulling at the bricks. They helped the people out and directed them away from the scene. Lindy and Reggie were the last to leave. 'Here, give me my boot back please Lindy.'

27
Bethany

The noise was deafening. The atmosphere was thick with filth. There was the "bof bof bof" sound of the anti-aircraft guns, the smell of fire was all around and the dust from the broken buildings was everywhere.

Thinking that their way was blocked up the hill to the main road to Whippingham, they turned towards the river. 'Maybe there is a foot path along the side,' suggested Reggie.

The tide was out and the water of the Medina River was low. On the other side they spotted a warship, firing consistently. They saw the men on the deck working hard reloading and firing. There were other sailors dropping buckets with rope attached, into the water, pulling them up to the ship and throwing water over the guns which were overheating with the work they were doing.

Everywhere the children went there were firemen with hoses, some of them were also manned by men in different uniforms and spoke a different language. These were sailors who were from the ship which was firing on the enemy. All their faces were covered in soot laden sweat.

They reached an area near the gas works, and suddenly, someone called. 'Reggie what are you doing here? Reggie! Reggie!'

Hearing his name, he turned and spotted his friend Colin from the fire station in Ryde. He went up to him. 'I came because I knew Lindy was here and I wanted to find her and take her home.'

'You shouldn't be here,' he shouted but Reggie couldn't hear and went closer. 'You must find shelter! This is very dangerous. Is that Lindy with you?'

'Yes, I found her!'

'They are attacking Cowes and East Cowes; for God's sake, you must find somewhere to shelter.'

'Can we get along the side of the river? Is there a path?'

'No, you'll have to go back up the hill and get to the main road. Stick together. Bert and I have been working at the gas works. The smell was awful.'

'We are off to the Tea Wagon for a break. I am looking forward to my cuppa.'

'Well deserved!' said Bert.

Women's Voluntary Service member, Mrs Hann had converted her husband's butcher's van so that she could serve tea to those working in the open. She had brought her van down nearer the action, so they didn't have to climb the hill.

'Such a nice lady,' said Colin

The two men were exhausted. 'Reggie! Lindy! you shouldn't be here. You need to find a shelter,' said Bert.

'Yes, he is right!' Colin added. 'We are very busy now. Take my advice and find some shelter. We must say goodbye now you two! Take Care.' With that they left, waved and walked smartly up the hill leaving Lindy and Reggie alone.

'Reggie,' shouted Lindy. 'Shall we go and find a shelter?'

'No let's get out of here!'

Colin and Bert were nowhere to be seen as Lindy and Reggie turned and quickly retraced their steps back towards the hill. They had just got around the corner when they heard a whistling sound. 'That's a bomb,' Reggie yelled as he pushed Lindy down onto the ground, which was already covered in bricks and debris.'

'Cover your ears,' yelled Reggie.

The children, buried their faces into the rubble and blocked their ears.

There was an enormous bang.

They lay still for a moment, and then they both reached out to each other.

Grabbing each other's hands, they breathed a sigh of relief, as they realised that they were both still alive.

'Stay still Lindy and check you are not injured,' said Reggie remembering his first aid training.

'No, I'm fine I think,' she said. 'We've been lucky! That was jolly close.'

'Jolly lucky,' said Reggie as he checked his limbs. Noticing more grazes he added, 'I've a few more war wounds on my legs though.' He laughed briefly.

Lindy did not respond to his joke. Her head remained buried in the bricks; she turned it sideways so her ear was near the earth.

'I think I can hear a child crying!' she said.

'What? Move over, let me listen.'

With their heads close together Reggie and Lindy lay flat on the rubble. They were lying so still that a warden from the A.R.P. who was passing by, thought they were dead.

'Hello!' he called. 'Hey can you hear me?' he shouted again.

'Shush!' said Lindy. 'We think we can hear a child crying.'

Taking his helmet off, the warden joined them, burying his head in the bricks like the children.

'My goodness you are right!' he said. 'It's a strong cry but I can only just hear it. Help me move the bricks, we can make a chain and pass them away from this area!'

They were soon joined by two ladies from the WVS and a red cross nurse. As the bricks were moved the sound of the crying got louder until the warden called stop.

The activity ceased, all remained quiet as the warden shone his torch into the hole. Then he put his head further into the gap that they had made.

'I can just see movement. There is definitely someone alive down there. There is a wooden beam, holding up the solidly built wall which had once been the side of the house.

And there was a space beneath. The gap is too small for me to climb through!'

The nurse came over and looked into the hole. 'I'm afraid it is too small for me to crawl through too,' she said. We are going to have to wait until we can get some heavy lifting gear to move the beam.'

Reggie crawled over to the hole and looked in. 'I could get through that!' he said.

'No! no!' said the warden, 'You are just a lad; we can't ask you to do that. How old are you?'

'I can, I can,' argued Reggie.

The warden spotted his uniform. 'Are you here as a messenger?'

'Well ... err ... yes, I suppose so.'

'Well as a messenger you need to take a message to get help and find someone to get a crane of some sort to lift that wall. There is a fire brigade lorry just down the road.'

'No! I can, I can do it!' pleaded Reggie.

The crying continued but the volume was weaker. The situation was obviously getting more urgent.

The nurse became more anxious. 'Let him do it, I don't think that child will last much longer.'

Reluctantly the warden agreed.

'I shall go in head first and crawl along until I am over the child. Then I'll reach down and pick the little one up.'

Reggie looked down the hole and with the aid of a torch from the ARP warden, he was able to see the pale pink blanket being kicked by the screaming child. With the aid of his scout scarf, he tied the warden's torch in the middle and then placed it on his head. He then tied the two ends together under his chin.

'It's alright, little one,' said Reggie in a soothing tone, 'I'm coming to get you.'

'Are you sure you really want to do this?' said the red cross nurse.

'Yeah, I can do it. She is quite deep down. I can slither in and I am sure I can reach her.'

The warden came over. 'He is certainly slim enough to get through that hole. But I don't know ... Should we allow him to do this? How old are you?'

'Old enough!' snapped Reggie, 'And I am a scout! There is a little girl in difficulties down there. I can do this. I can get her out!'

The crying ceased. The situation now had become dire, so the decision was made.

'We need to get the child rescued and out of that collapsed building as quickly as possible,' said the warden. 'I have a rope, I can tie it around your waist and hold on to it, just in case you have to go deeper than you had thought.'

'What makes you think it is a girl?' said Lindy

'Pink blanket of course,' said Reggie. Still kneeling on the rubble, he stretched up and put his hands on his hips. 'A Scout whistles and is cheerful under all difficulties,' Reggie whispered to himself. But Lindy heard.

'I'll whistle for you!' she said.

Reggie lay on the bricks his head near the hole he was to crawl through. The warden tied the rope around his waist.

'Are you sure you want to do this? You don't have to.'

Reggie disregarded that question. He obviously didn't want to do it, but there was a child under the rubble who should not be there, and he needed to get the child out.

'I'm ready,' said Reggie and using his arms and legs he crawled into the hole and under the debris. Lindy stood by and tried to whistle for him, but couldn't, her mouth was too dry.

'What are you doing?' asked the Nurse.

'Trying to whistle!' she replied. 'A Scout whistles and is cheerful under all difficulties! Reggie can't whistle, so I said I would whistle for him.'

'I'll whistle for him too,' said the Nurse.

Lindy, the two nurses and the ARP warden lay flat on the bricks listening to Reggie who was under the debris. They whistled alternately and the sound of whistling gave Reggie more courage as he crawled further into the hole. 'I'm coming for you little one,' he said.

'Are you alright lad?' asked the ARP man.

'Yep!' came the reply. 'I think I will need an extra rope; she is further in than I reckoned.'

'OK lad! I'm on to that.'

'His name is Reggie,' said Lindy

'Is he your brother?' asked the nurse.

'No. We are evacuees and good friends.'

Suddenly above the noise of the guns and explosions, they managed to hear Reggie call out, 'I can nearly reach her! Hello little one! Come to Reggie. You will be safe now.'

The beam had landed across a sturdy chest of drawers which protected the high-sided cot. The toddler looked unharmed.

He reached forward, put his hands under her arms and picked up the little girl with the pink blanket. Holding her across his chest with his left arm, he prepared himself to get out. There was no room to turn around, so he decided he would have to go out feet first.

'Can you help by pulling the rope carefully,' called Reggie.

'Yes, I will,' said the warden. 'I'll keep the rope tight, and tighten it as you move towards me.'

Reggie held the child across his chest making sure his left hand cradled her head.

'Are you ready?' shouted the warden.

'Yes,' said Reggie, as he started to crawl backwards. The action of moving his legs and one arm over the rubble and bricks he grazed his skin. When he squeezed through the smaller spaces, he caught his shirt on the various jagged bricks, splintered wood and rubble creating holes in his scout shirt as he went.

As the warden felt the rope slacken, he adjusted it accordingly, and kept it tight as Reggie moved.

Slowly and carefully, Reggie and the little girl inched their way out of the hole.

What a joy for Lindy when Reggie's boots appeared through the bricks, followed by his body until Lindy saw the back of his head covered with his scout scarf. When he was clear from the obstruction he rolled over and sat up on the bricks, still cuddling the child who was nestled in his arms. His scarf and torch had managed to stay on his head.

'There you are precious! You are safe now,' he said and almost reluctantly, handed over the bundle to the red cross nurse. On the corner of the blanket there was some embroidery. Reggie reached for the torch on his head. He took it off and shone the light on to the blanket where he spotted the word 'Bethany' embroidered with neat stitches.

'So, you are Bethany,' said Reggie as he handed her over to the Red Cross Nurse.

After undoing the rope around his waist, Reggie stood up. His legs were covered with blood and more grazes where they had scraped along the debris as he crawled in and then out of what was left of the house. The warden came up to him and the two stood face to face.

'My goodness, that was such a brave thing you have done!' The two men shook hands.

Reggie shook out his scarf and replaced it around his neck fastening it with his woggle which he had safely stowed in his pocket. He handed the torch back to the warden.

'Well done,' said Lindy.

'How is the little girl?' asked Reggie.

The nurse held the bundle of child and blanket. Bethany was very still.

'Oh err ... she is asleep,' said the nurse realising that she was talking to a child. 'Yes, asleep Reggie.'

'Unconscious?' mouthed the ARP warden. The nurse's response was a gentle nod of her head.

Bethany was whisked away in an ambulance with the Red Cross nurses, the ARP man disappeared and Lindy and Reggie were left alone.

As they walked up the hill, they passed the place where they had expected to see the tea waggon. But there was no tea waggon, no WVS lady, and no Colin or Bert, just piles of bricks, pieces of wood, bits of a van and broken pieces of furniture.

'I thought it was here,' said Reggie.

'No time to look now, we must get going,' said Lindy.

They walked for a while; Reggie kept a look out for places to shelter. They had to duck and dive under hedges and walls, as the aircraft flew overhead. They heard bullets hit the ground around them. The air was filled with the smell of explosives, burning buildings and brick dust. It was easy to see where they were heading as the light from the fires lit the area as bright as day.

They got to the top of the hill. The hedge around Osborne House was in front of them.

'Good,' said Reggie that hedge will give us cover. 'We won't be seen under there.'

As the children walked on in the early hours of the morning, they did not know but the last bomb that had fallen very close to them obliterated the tea wagon, killing the firemen Colin and Bert and Mrs Hann the WVS Tea Lady.

28
The House at Whippingham

Lindy and Reggie allowed themselves a short rest under the hedge outside Osborne House. After a while they got up and started trudging along the road, when suddenly they heard the obvious sound of gun shots, "ratter tat, tat." It came from the machine guns on the planes which sounded very close.

'Get down!' shouted Reggie. 'He is firing at us.' They dived for the ground again, and covered their ears as they pushed their faces into the earth. The firing stopped, but there was another explosion nearby. Earth, stones and broken bricks rained down on the children. They both screamed, but there was no-one to hear them. They lay still waiting for a lull in the attack.

Lindy lifted her head and looked around. She could still hear explosions, but they were further away.

'They must have run out of bullets,' said Lindy. 'That's a relief! Come on Reggie let's walk on further. We are nearly at Whippingham it won't be as bad there ... I hope!'

Reggie lay still on the ground. For one ghastly moment, she thought he had been hit.

'**Reggie,**' she yelled. '**Reggie, Reggie!**'

He moved and got up. 'Stop teasing me! you made me really scared,' said Lindy. 'I thought you were dead!'

Reggie said nothing. He just took Lindy's hand and started to walk along the road. She suddenly became aware that his hand was shaking.

'Are you alright?' she asked.

He looked at her vacantly, as if he didn't know who she was. Then he looked at his arms and then down his shirt.

'I've torn my shirt!' he said.

Instinctively Lindy loosed her hand from his and put her arm comfortingly around his back. 'Oh Reggie, we'll be alright, we are together,' she said. Then she took his hand again.

'Don't worry about your shirt, Cludgy will mend it. Come on Reggie,' she said calmly as she could above the noise and chaos. 'We are going to be alright! We are going home.'

'My shirt is torn! I've torn my shirt.'

Lindy suddenly became very frightened, but having to comfort and support her friend she found some strength.

'Look it's getting brighter. We'll soon find safety somewhere. There will be blue skies over us again. It won't always be like this forever.'

They turned left after they had passed the school, to take the shorter route to Wootton.

'A short cut!' said Lindy. 'We are taking the short cut. It won't be long now.'

'My shirt is torn,' muttered Reggie. 'It's all torn!'

'Shush Reggie, Cludgy will mend your shirt,' said Lindy. 'Shush now, save your breath for walking.'

Reggie remained silent as they walked together. They found a rhythm to their steps to the tune that Lindy was humming.

'What is that tune?' she asked herself. 'I think it is "All Things Bright and Beautiful." That's right!' she answered. 'So, it is. Reggie, are you feeling a bit better?'

Reggie didn't have time to answer, as he fell into a pot hole at the side of the road. 'Reggie! Oh Reggie!' she said.

Lindy was nearly at the end of her tether. 'How am I going to cope with all this?' she said to herself. Suddenly she remembered how her mother had taught her to be brave. Then she said out loud. 'You are strong! You will manage', it was as if she heard her mother say those words. Lindy stood up tall and shouted. 'I can, I shall, and **I will**!'

'Come on Reggie, it's only a graze; you brag about your war wounds. Now you have another.'

With Lindy's help Reggie stood up. 'Put your arm over my shoulders, and we can walk together like that.'

There was no rhythm to their progress now. Reggie had hurt his knee and twisted his ankle. They staggered on and at the bend in the road they saw a Victorian villa.

'I'm going to knock on that front door and ask for some water,' Lindy announced.

They stumbled up the path and went into the porch. She knocked on the door; they waited! The door was eventually opened by a tall man dressed in an over coat.

'Excuse me sir,' she said. 'We have walked from East Cowes, and I would be grateful for a glass of water ... please?'

'Oh, my goodness! Come in! Come in! Doris! Doris! come quickly and give me a hand. We have just come in from our garden shelter.'

'What is it, George?' said his wife.

What a sorry sight greeted the owners of the house. The two friends' clothes were covered in brick dust, bits of hedge where they had lain and dirt from the road. Reggie's uniform shirt was torn, and both of his legs were covered in grazes and blood. Lindy's school uniform at first glance had survived the ordeal but was filthy. She still had her school hat; it had been stuffed in her pocket.

George took Reggie's free arm and put it over his shoulder, together with Lindy, they helped him into the sitting room. 'We'll put him on the sofa.'

So much attention was being given to Reggie that Lindy was left standing in the middle of the room. She was beginning to feel sick and a little giddy.

'Sit down my dear,' said Doris. 'Take the comfy chair near the fire, I will put a log on the embers, and hope it takes light.'

The giddiness left her, but the sickness prevailed. 'Please may I have a drink of water?'

Doris disappeared and quickly returned with a glass of water for Lindy, which she drank greedily. It revived her! 'Thank you so much! We are sorry to be such a nuisance.'

'Don't worry! Don't worry at all!' said George.

'No not at all,' said Doris, as she gave a blanket to Lindy and laid another one over Reggie. 'I think those leg injuries need to be attended to.'

'I'll revive the fire,' said George.

Doris returned with a bowl of warm water and proceeded to bathe Reggie's wounds. The soothing sound and action of the warm water as it flowed over Reggie's legs was enough to lull the travellers into a sleep.

'My first aid box is a little lacking in bandages but I think I can find something for these. You have been in the wars, haven't you?'

There was no reply. George returned to the sitting room carrying more logs which he laid in the hearth.

'That'll keep the fire going,' he said.

Doris roused Reggie and persuaded him to drink some water. He did not drink much, as he fell back to sleep quickly.

Doris and George sat in their sitting room watching over the two young travellers as they recovered from their ordeal. 'What shall we do next?' said George. He paused deep in thought. 'I think we should try and get them home. I don't think the young boy's injuries are life threatening.'

'But we don't know where they live,' said Doris. 'Or what their names are for that matter.'

'They are sleeping soundly. Let's leave them for the time being.'

'I'll make some tea,' said Doris. They decided that they would remain with them in case they needed something.

Doris returned with a teapot, a milk jug, two cups and saucers. The smell of the tea and the noise of the tea being poured awoke Lindy.

'Hello, sleepy head,' said George. 'Would you like a cup of tea? Take mine, I'll get another cup. Do you take sugar?'

'No thank you, I don't,' Lindy said, 'but I would love a cup of tea.' She sat up as George passed her the cup and saucer.

'Now you can tell us all about yourself,' said Doris. 'What are your names; where do you come from and what on earth were you doing in East Cowes, on a night like this!'

Between sips of tea Lindy recounted. 'My name is Lindy Elliot, and my friend is Reggie Mitchell. We live by the church in Little Bridge. I live with Cludgy and Arthur Sparrow.'

'Gosh I know Cludgy and Arthur. We used to go to the Quays for weekend parties. How are they? Cludgy used to make divine cakes!'

'Oh, she still makes cakes, when she can get enough fat, flour and sugar.'

'Don't you need eggs?'

'Yes, but they keep six chickens.'

George returned from the kitchen carrying his cup and a piece of buttered toast, which he gave to Lindy.'

'Gosh, thank you! Are you sure you don't need that for yourself.'

'I thought you would enjoy it. Build up your strength. I had wanted to put jam on it, but we have run out.'

'Cludgy has some, she makes it in the summer.' Lindy devoured her toast and drank her tea.

'With all this talk about cakes, I have just remembered it was my school friend Clarissa's birthday yesterday. I was spending the night at her house. Then the raid started and we got separated when we were going to the shelter. Oh, my goodness, I wonder where she is.'

'There is nothing you can do about finding her now,' said Doris. 'I suspect she is as concerned about you, as you are about her. You cannot go back and look for her now, and she cannot go out and look for you either. Let us hope she is safe and you'll see her later.'

'At school hopefully,' said Lindy.

As they sipped their tea, the all clear sounded. It was a quarter past six.

'Now we must get you home,' said Doris.

'I've been thinking about that,' said George. 'How would you like a ride in a cart, pulled by my Welsh cobb horse, Sergeant.'

Lindy's eyes lit up. 'Thank you, that would be lovely. I've not ridden in a horse drawn cart before.'

'I'll finish my tea,' said George, 'and go and get the cart ready and persuade Sergeant to come out of his field.'

'I hope he doesn't play up and comes when you call,' said Doris. 'He's a big fellow, and despite his size he can move quite quickly. Not as fast as our lovely car. It's a Wolseley Wasp, but we have no fuel for that so we have had to leave it in the garage.'

They finished their tea and Doris took the tray back to the kitchen. George disappeared outside to get Sergeant and the cart ready to drive to Little Bridge.

Lindy sat staring at the embers and soon drifted off to sleep again. She was woken by Reggie, suddenly shouting in his sleep.

She jumped up and rushed over to him. He was crying and thrashing his arms and legs about.

'It's all right Reggie!' called Lindy. 'You are safe here. We are both safe.'

'I've torn my shirt!' he yelled. 'My scout shirt!'

Doris hearing the commotion joined Lindy and stroked Reggie's forehead. 'Reggie you are fine, you are safe!'

After about five minutes, Reggie stopped yelling and sat calmly on the sofa staring at the fire.

'A nightmare,' said Doris. 'What on earth happened to you in East Cowes?'

'Oh, nothing really,' Lindy lied, as she really didn't want to talk about it.

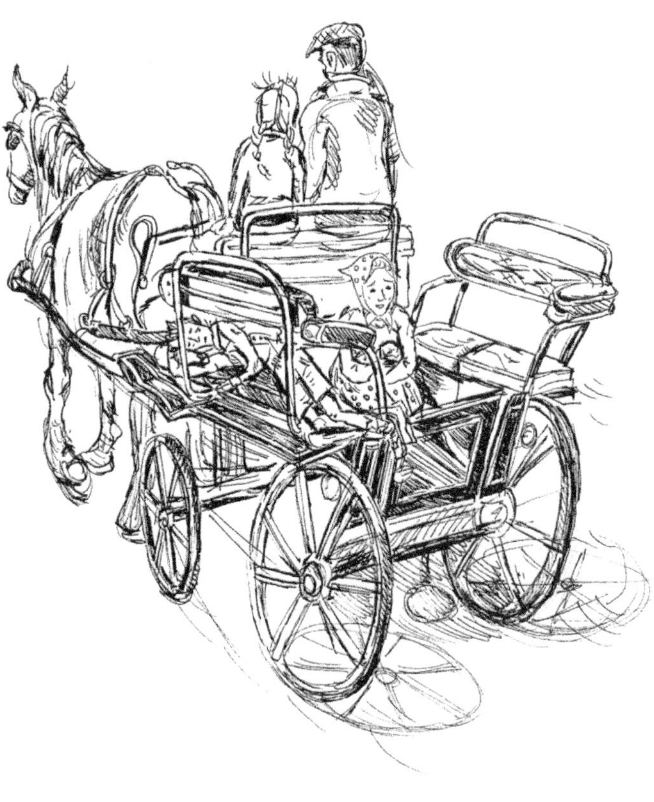

29
A Ride Home in Style

Persuading Sergeant that he wanted to have an outing from his field and take Lindy and Reggie home took longer than expected. He kept standing still, enticing George to come closer, and then when he was just a yard away, too far to catch his halter, he neighed and galloped off.

'How did you persuade him in the end?' asked Doris back at the house.

'A piece of carrot,' said George. 'It was a bit mouldy, it had been in my pocket a long time, but he fell for the bribe.' With his bridle on, he tied him to the ring on the wall in the yard, where he waited patiently. George returned to the house.

'Doris!' he called, 'Where is the key to the tack room?'

'When did you last have it?'

'When I went to the shops on Saturday.'

'Well, I guess that they are in the pocket of your green jacket because that is what you wore on Saturday.'

'But I am wearing my green jacket.'

'Well then I bet it is there.'

He slipped both hands into his pockets and found the key. 'Funny I didn't find it when I found that mouldy carrot for Sergeant.'

'Funny that!' repeated is wife. 'Now, Sergeant is waiting in the yard, for you to harness him up ready for the trip.'

'Lindy we must wake Reggie up, and give him a bit of sustenance.'

'Sustenance?' asked Lindy.

'Yes, that's right,' said Doris. 'Hot buttered toast, and a cup of tea with some sugar in it. You wake him and I'll make the toast.'

Reggie did feel a lot better after his impromptu meal. He did not remember his nightmare at all.

'My uniform!' he said. 'I've torn my shirt. How did that happen?'

Lindy did not pursue an answer to that question, rather she said, 'Won't Cludgy and Arthur be surprised when they see us arrive in a cart pulled by a horse?' said Lindy.

'Sergeant is a Welsh Cobb,' said George. 'He is strong and very reliable.'

'Now Reggie I am going to support you. I'll hold your arm,' said Doris.

'I'll take the other arm,' said Lindy.

'And we will help you to go out to the yard.' Usually, Reggie would argue when questioned as to his ability to do anything, he would say he could manage. But he didn't, he said nothing but with their help managed to walk. They turned the corner of the house and found the stables.

Despite being warned they were a little shocked at the size of the animal in front of them.

'Isn't he tall,' said Lindy.

'I've worked with taller horses,' said George. 'Sergeant pulls this wagonette. You should meet Major he pulls large hay carts.'

Sergeant was black. His mane flowed over his shoulders. His tail was combed and nearly reached the floor. He had a blaze of white down his face.

'I bet you have fun combing all that hair,' said Lindy.

'We are very busy running the farm, but I still find time to pamper Sergeant.' said George. 'It's important to look after our working horses, they play an important part on the farm. We were thinking of buying a tractor in the autumn of 1938. But with the prospect of a war looming, and the thought that petrol would be rationed, we changed our minds.'

So that their introduction to Sergeant would go smoothly, the children had been armed with a piece of apple to give him. Lindy could only just touch his nose with her arm outstretched. Sergeant lowered his head to reach Reggie's piece.

In the early morning light, the children could just see the waggonette. It was black and shiny. There was a bench seat facing forwards at the front of the vehicle for the driver and one other. Behind this were two further bench seats facing each other designed to take four. 'There is plenty of room for you two in the back,' said George. 'The seats are well padded, so you should be comfortable.'

Lindy was ready to climb on board when she suddenly remembered Reggie, who was not his usual self. She turned around to help, but George and Doris had their arms under Reggie's shoulders and helped him up into the cart. Lindy stood waiting.

'Can you manage Lindy?' asked George.

'Oh yes!' she said. 'I was waiting to see if you needed me to help with Reggie.' Lindy climbed into the back of the waggonette.

'There are two blankets for you both,' Doris said. 'Wrap them around you, and keep warm.'

Reggie picked up the blanket and looked at it not knowing what he had to do with it.

'Here Reggie,' said Lindy. 'Let me help you.' She laid it open on the bench. 'Now sit on top of it.' When he had sat down, Lindy wrapped over the two sides over Reggie's lower body and his bruised and battered legs.

Swiftly and deftly, George hopped onto their carriage and into his seat at the front. At the command of 'Sergeant Walk On,' Sergeant shuffled his feet and walked forward slowly. George, with the aid of his long whip, touched the horse on his left side and the horse turned. 'Left, go left,' he said. With continuous command to go left, eventually the horse and carriage turned completely around to face the other way.

After locking the front door, Doris joined them. 'Are we all ready?' she said.

'Yes. We are just waiting for you.'

Doris ran down to the large gate at the front of the property and opened it.

'Sergeant. Walk on!' said George. Sergeant obliged and slowly walked through the open space left by the large five barred gate. They waited on the other side, whilst Doris shut the gate behind her. Then equally skilfully as her husband had been, she climbed aboard and sat next to him.

'Sergeant, walk on!' said George.

At first the road was smooth and the ride was pleasant and George was able to go a little faster.

'Sergeant, terr … rot,' he said. The horse dutifully trotted along the open road.

They turned a bend and Sergeant stopped. We have a small hill to go down. 'Hold on tight everyone,' said George, 'at the bottom of this there is a small ditch to negotiate. The authorities are not interested in mending small ditches, they are too busy mending big holes created by the enemy.'

'Sergeant, walk on,' said George. The horse knew this spot and slowly and carefully pulled the wagon over the obstacle. The passengers lurched forwards and sideways. Reggie who had been sitting upright during the ride, suddenly fell forwards. Lindy saw him, and leant towards him as he fell on her.

'Mrs Doris!' she called. 'Reggie can't sit up anymore.'

George stopped the cart.

'Alright, I'm coming,' said Doris as she jumped down from her seat. Reggie stirred. 'Let's get him in a more comfortable position.'

Doris and Lindy moved him so he was laying down on the bench. 'He needs a pillow,' said Doris as she took off her jacket and rolled it up. Trying to stretch out his legs Reggie hit the simple metal hand rail at the end. It was made of a single strand thus creating a space. Lindy took his bruised, battered and bandaged legs one by one and threaded them through the hole. He did look funny with his legs sticking out of the cart.

'That's a good idea,' said Doris. 'Now Lindy you go up front with George and I'll stay in the back with Reggie in case he rolls off the bench. She folded the blanket and tucked it around as much of his body as she could. It was impossible that his feet and lower legs could be covered. They had to remain protruding out the back.

'Steady Sergeant, stand still now,' said George.

Lindy climbed out and went around to the front. 'Well young lady, let me tell you how to get in.'

Lindy stood still and listened.

'Firstly, you put your right foot on the middle of the wheel, push up on that leg and then put your left foot on the little step in front of the wheel, finally put your right foot in the cab. Do you think you can manage that?'

'Yes, I think so,' said Lindy. She looked at the wheel and the little step and talked to herself as to how she was to do the manoeuvre. Then very competently she put her right foot up, then added her left foot to the step, and finally put her right foot onto the carriage.

Doris passed her the rug she had been using. 'Wrap that around you it tends to be colder at the front.'

Now without her coat or a blanket Doris sat on the floor between the seats just in case Reggie should fall from the bench onto the floor. 'If I snuggle down behind the drivers cab, I am out of the wind,' she said.

'Are you alright my dear?' said George.

'Yes, I'm fine, stop worrying George,' said Doris.

Up in the driver's cab, Lindy shivered. 'Wrap the blanket over you and lean against me,' said George. Lindy moved herself nearer to him. 'Are we all ready to go?' he said.

'Yes,' said Doris from the back.

'Yes,' said Lindy.

'Sergeant … walk on,' said George.

Sergeant obeyed. With George's guidance and Sergeants' skill, the waggonette travelled along over the rough ground to where the smooth road lay ahead.

Once on the main road, George and Sergeant were able to relax. 'Sergeant. Terr … rot.' Lindy became more at ease with the steady rhythm of the horse's hooves clip clopping on the road.

'Time for a story,' said George. 'Would you like a story, Lindy?'

'Yes please,' said Lindy.

'Yes please,' echoed Doris from the back who was sat on the floor of the waggonette her knees cuddled up to her chest. 'Right! Are you sitting comfortably, then I'll begin,' he said.

'Once upon a time, a great queen used to live in a large house called Osbourne. She owned a waggonette a little like this one. It was smaller and called a half waggonette. She used to ride in it, pulled along by a Shetland Pony, who took her all around the enormous gardens that surrounded the big house. Well ... at the beginning of this century, 40 years ago, she died and the waggonette was put aside and not used.

'A milkman, called Fred, needed a cart to take his milk around the houses. They looked everywhere, but the ones they found were either too big, too small, or they were in such a poor condition so as to be not strong enough. Fred owned a horse, Mary, but she was not robust enough to pull a very heavy vehicle. Fred thought of asking a local farmer if he could borrow his large cart horse. But he decided not to ask, as the cart horse was already very busy on the farm, doing essential work providing food for the nation. He also decided that feeding him would cost too much, thus reducing his profits.

'A friend of a friend of Fred's heard about his plight. "I know where there is a cart that would suit you and your horse, Mary, admirably. It belonged to Queen Victoria," he told Fred. "It's at the back of the stables. Shall I ask if we can go and see it?"

"Yes please," said Fred. So, a meeting was set up and Fred went to see the half waggonette.

'They found it under a dust sheet, hidden at the back of the stable block. They had to move a lot of boxes and other debris to get to it. When they got it free from its prison, they pulled off the dust sheet and revealed the compact waggonette. "She's a little dusty, but she is sound," said the man from Osbourne. "Her majesty would have insisted on that. What do you need it for?"

"I have nothing in which to deliver my milk," he said. Fred recognised that the man from Osbourne house was a little reticent.

"It is work of national importance," he said. "It is essential that I get my milk to my customers. To the families and their children." I think it was the word 'children' that swung the decision.

"Well alright then, if it is work of national importance then you must have it."

'So, the little half waggonette was commandeered, and with the help from Mary, his horse, he delivers milk to his customers.'

George finished the story speaking alone, as his audience, Lindy, Doris and Reggie were all asleep.

30
Home

It was seven o'clock in the early morning that Auntie Bee woke up and realised something was wrong. She had not heard Reggie return from delivering his message.

'Robert, Robert! Wake up! Reggie's not in.' Robert stirred and opened his eyes. 'What! Staying out all night? I'll have to have words with him about this behaviour. He really is a naughty boy.'

Bee ran next door to Cludgy's house. She banged on the door furiously and shouted, 'Reggie is not home! He did not come back last night.'

Cludgy leapt out of bed and rushed to the window, she pulled down the blackouts and looked at the clock.

'Arthur, wake up! something is wrong,' she yelled.

'Do you know what time it is?' said Arthur.

'It's getting on for half past seven!' said Cludgy

Arthur lifted his head from the pillow. 'Yes, so it is, I had a late shift which finished at four thirty; I've only just got to bed.'

'Be serious Arthur, Bee is outside. She sounds frantic!'

Cludgy quickly dressed, rushed downstairs and opened the kitchen door.

'Come in, come in,' said Cludgy. 'Whatever is the matter?'

'Reggie is not home yet. I saw him late last night. He took Lindy's bike and cycled off telling me he was a messenger and had to deliver a document.'

'Where was he going?' asked Cludgy.

'I don't know, he didn't tell me, he just cycled off at top speed.'

'Come and sit down, I'll put the kettle on and we'll have some tea.'

Arthur appeared in the kitchen.

'I thought I left you fast asleep Arthur,' said Cludgy. 'You have only just got to bed. What was going on last night?'

'There was a raid on Cowes and East Cowes.'

Cludgy gasped and flopped down into a chair, 'Oh no! oh my goodness Lindy went to East Cowes to stay with her friend Clarissa.'

'There is no reason that we should believe that she was caught up in this,' said Arthur. 'Let's not worry, and as for Reggie, he was at training last night at the fire station, why should we think that his message was something to do with Cowes. These messengers go to lots of other fire stations, Bembridge for instance. So, let's keep calm.'

The ladies paused, Bee found a handkerchief in her pocket of her dressing gown, and wiped her eyes. Cludgy felt sick, and was as white as a sheet.

'No news is good news,' said Arthur.

Cludgy and Bee turned and looked at him. 'That is no help,' said Cludgy.

'I hate that proverb,' said Bee. 'It means absolutely nothing and is no comfort at all.' She burst into tears again.

The kettle boiled and the water was poured into the tea pot.

'I hope the milk is alright, this came yesterday,' said Cludgy. 'It's too early for the milk to arrive today. He comes at about eight.' *Why am I worrying about the milk when Lindy and Reggie are missing?* she thought.

There were no words of explanation that would comfort Bee.

'I don't think William is at home either,' said Cludgy, 'I'll go to Smugglers Cottage and find out. She ran along the lane and banged on the door. 'William, are you in there?' Pushing open the door she called again. The door to his bedroom was ajar, so she looked in. The bed was made, and had not been slept in. She turned and left. As she ran back, she heard the sound of horse's hooves on the road.

'Whatever is that?' she said as she walked up the lane to the church. Not knowing what it was, she stood still and listened. *We don't get horses down this lane. Especially not at this time in the morning. Whatever is going on?'* She thought.

She walked further up the road towards the sound just as a horse and trap came around the corner. There was a man waving at her from the seat at the front, and next to him was a lump covered by a blanket. George had recognised Cludgy immediately. As she got closer, she saw two sandaled feet sticking out of the blanket.

'Good morning Cludgy,' George yelled out. 'I have got two passengers for you. Yes, they are both here!' The bundle in the front seat moved as Lindy pushed back the blanket from her face. As her eyes opened, she suddenly recognised Cludgy.

'Oh Cludgy!' she said, and then 'Cludgy,' she yelled. 'Oh, Cludgy I am so glad to see you.'

Cludgy rushed up to her. 'Oh, thank God!' she stretched up to reach her.

'Slow down young lady,' said George. 'You must take care when you are getting down from my waggonette.'

'Oh yes! I remember.' Lindy said, then she paused and thought how to do it. Its left foot on the step, right foot on the centre of the wheel, then left leg on the road.

Cludgy and Lindy were now able to put their arms around each other. Hearing the commotion, Arthur, Auntie Bee and Robert came out of the cottage and walked up the lane.

'Cludgy, Reggie is hurt,' said Lindy. They released their hold and went around the back.

Auntie Bee, Arthur and George rushed around to the back of the waggonette, where they discovered Reggie lying on one of the benches and Doris cuddled up on the floor in between them. She lifted her head up, yawned and said, 'Good morning, everyone.'

Cludgy recognised her immediately.

'Doris!' she shouted. 'Good heavens! Good morning, Doris! What on earth are you doing here? And how did Lindy and Reggie get a lift home in your pony and cart.'

'It's a waggonette not a cart,' said Doris. And it's a long story. They are a little worse for wear, but alright I feel. I think they have a lot to tell you.'

In the back of the waggonette lay Reggie, still fast asleep, lying on a bench under a blanket with his bandaged and bloodied legs sticking out through the hole at the end.

'We must get him out and carry him into the house,' said Cludgy.

Doris stood up ready to take his shoulders. It looked to Lindy as if Doris was going to pull him upwards thus freeing his legs.

'No, no, you must undo his legs first!' said Lindy. 'I put them like that.'

Slowly and carefully, she took each injured leg and unthreaded them through the gap, avoiding touching the sides. Then she put his feet onto the floor. Once they were free, Reggie, now awake, sat up.

'Hello Lindy,' he said. 'I've torn my shirt.'

'Yes, I know. Cludgy's here and she'll mend it. Won't you Cludgy?'

'Of course, my pet. That's no trouble, no trouble at all.'

Supported by Arthur and Auntie Bee, Reggie climbed down onto the road. He was very weak and his knees buckled under him. Fortunately, Arthur was holding him under his shoulders so he didn't fall. It was obvious that Auntie Bee was too small to give him the support he needed. Suddenly from nowhere Robert in his pyjamas rushed forward and took his wife's place. Together they supported Reggie back to Robert and Auntie Bee's cottage.

'Take him through to the sitting room?' said Auntie Bee, 'and lay him on the sofa.'

Cludgy fetched a bowl of water and knelt down on the floor by the sofa. 'I'll just have a look at your war wounds,' she said. Reggie did not react. He used to be proud of his injuries from trips and falls often caused by incidents involving football.

His legs and arms were covered with grazes some of them were covered with bandages. His shirt was badly torn and his face was filthy. He couldn't stop shaking and kept repeating that his shirt was torn. He squealed every time Cludgy moved a bandage. 'Some of these grazes are quite deep. I think we need a doctor,' said Cludgy.

'I'll go,' said Lindy, 'I can ride my bike to his house, I know where he lives.'

'No, you can't,' said Auntie Bee.

'I can,' she insisted. 'I can ride my bike well and go really quickly! Much faster than Reggie on his small one!'

'No, you can't,' repeated Auntie Bee. 'Reggie borrowed your bike last night.'

This was the last straw for Lindy, she couldn't help her friend anymore. He needed a doctor and she couldn't cycle to get one. She ran to Cludgy, who still was kneeling on the floor, she sunk down, clung on to her and broke down in floods of tears.

'I can't help him anymore,' she wailed.

'It's alright Lindy. There is another way.' She turned to Bee. 'Can you find someone to go around to the rectory and ask Reverend Peterson if we can use his phone. All will be well Lindy. Trust me, all will be well.'

It was at this point Cludgy realised that there were two casualties and Lindy needed her attention. When Auntie Bee returned, she took over bathing Reggie's legs. 'I'll do that Cludgy, you take Lindy next door.'

'We must get you home Lindy my pet. You need a bath, something to eat and a good sleep.'

Robert was happy to take a brisk walk around to the vicarage.

'But you are still in your pyjamas,' said Auntie Bee.

'I know, but Reggie is more important. Won't be long.'

George drove the cart further down the lane and gently manoeuvred Sergeant to turn around completely, ready to drive home.

'Come into the cottage and refresh yourself said Arthur, 'I'll get a bucket of water for Sergeant. He could possibly do with a rest.'

George parked the waggonette in the lane. He put some blocks behind each wheel to prevent the vehicle from rolling backwards down the hill. Arthur returned with the water which he gave Sergeant.

'Is that all he needs?' Arthur asked George. 'He won't take off on his own, will he?'

'No,' said George, 'Sergeant and I have been good partners for many years; he's a patient horse. Except of course, when he is in his field, then he can be a devil to catch.'

Everyone was so relieved to see Lindy and Reggie home they gave very little attention to what happened in Cowes. A jam sandwich and a mug of hot milk and honey was prepared for Lindy.

'I don't think I am hungry Cludgy,' said Lindy.

'That's because you are very tired. Try and eat what you can. I'm going to run you a bath. You'll feel much better after a warm soak.'

She ate slowly and before she knew it, had finished the meal and was ready for her bath.

Lindy began to talk a bit whilst she was relaxing in the warm water, and told Cludgy brief disjointed tales of what happen.

'What's wrong with Reggie? He was so brave. Why is he so worried about his shirt being torn?'

'I don't really know. Perhaps it was all too much for him.'

'Can you mend it? I told him lots of times that you could.'

'I've not really looked at it, but I am pretty sure I can.'

'You are just so clever Cludgy.'

'Well, I don't know about that. Anyway, the doctor will be here soon, I hope. He'll help him get better.'

Cludgy helped Lindy into a clean nightdress and tucked her into bed.

'Good night, Lindy, or should I say good morning!'

Lindy smiled.

Downstairs in the kitchen, Doris, George and Arthur were sipping tea, when Robert popped his head around the door.

'The doctor's wife said he is not in, and last night he was called over to East Cowes Town Hall to help the Royal Army Medical Corps. Apparently, they were inundated with casualties.'

'I heard that there was a massive raid over there,' said Arthur.

'We spent the night in our shelter,' said George.

'The noise was frightening,' said Doris.

'And Reggie and Lindy were in the thick of it,' said Arthur.

'Thank God they are safe now,' said Doris.

They all agreed. 'But I am worried about Reggie,' said Cludgy. 'He seems fixated on his scout shirt being torn.'

George and Doris finished their tea. 'Thank you for the refreshment! We certainly needed that. We must make our way home now. We have a bit of gardening to do. It's surprising just how quick the weeds take over when they have been left for only a few days.'

'Thank you so much,' said Doris.

'But more importantly,' added Cludgy, 'We must thank you for taking the children in and bringing them home.'

31
Recovery

Dr O'Brien was finally able to call to see Reggie on Wednesday. There were so many casualties in West and East Cowes, that he stayed longer than expected.

'Reggie's wounds,' said the doctor, 'will heal in time. Especially in a healthy lad like Reggie. However, it's the wounds inside his head that will take longer.'

'He talks in his sleep. How can I help?' said Auntie Bee.

'Patience, you must be patient. Give him lots of love.'

'He had a dreadful nightmare last night! It was hard to wake him.'

'Ah yes, that will happen,' replied the doctor. 'During the great war, young men who before going to France were strong both physically and mentally, signed up feeling that they could do something for their country, they could fight ... and win. After the fighting a lot of them came home unable to function. They were not able to do much at all. Some shook quite violently and uncontrollably; it was named shell shock. Reggie has experienced real war, bombs falling, explosions and gun fire. However, he has youth on his side. He lives in quiet surroundings, discounting of course the planes flying overhead.'

'So, what can I do?' Auntie Bee repeated.

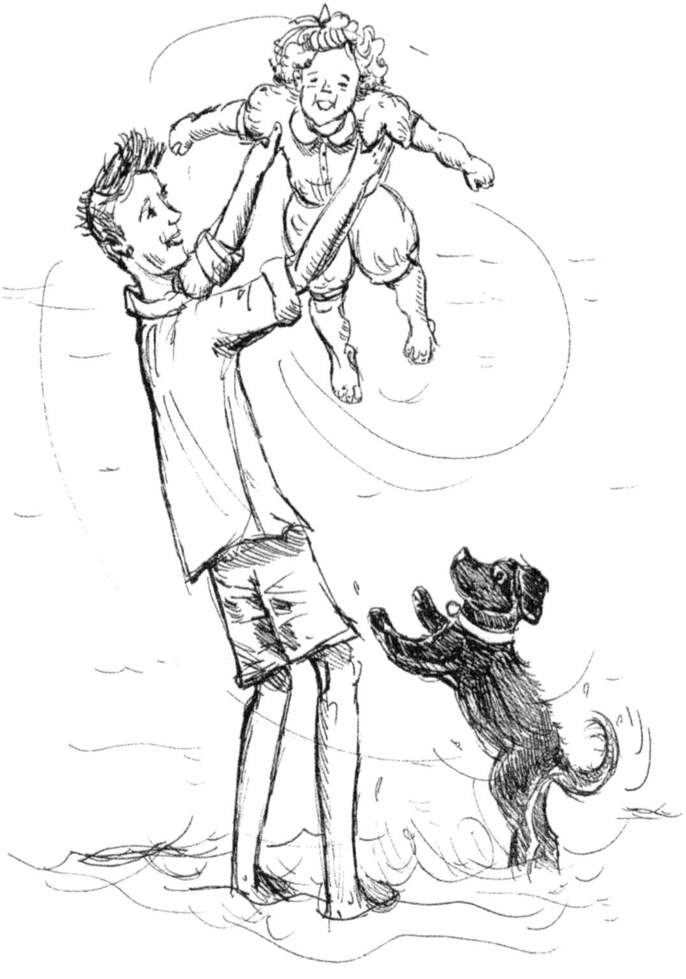

'Make life as normal as possible! Give him good food. Let him wander outside in the fields, woods and on the beach. God willing, he will be able to overcome this.'

'He likes drawing and painting.'

'That's good. Encourage that, he may be able to express his feelings onto the paper, whereas now he feels he can't tell you directly.'

Lindy called just as the doctor was leaving.

'Look!' she shouted, 'Look what I have got. Is Reggie in? Cludgy has mended Reggie's scout shirt.' Lindy held it up by the shoulders to show them. 'You can hardly see where it was torn.'

Auntie Bee did not want to ruin Lindy's excitement, but could not be as enthusiastic as Lindy was.

'Come in Lindy, I must talk to you quite seriously.' They sat in the kitchen and Auntie Bee explained to Lindy everything that Dr O'Brien had said. She listened and remembered how she was Reggie's constant companion when he had learned that his father was missing. She knew what to do.

'I'll be there with him,' she told Auntie Bee. 'You can rely on me.'

'Yes, I know I can. You are a true loyal friend.'

During the next few weeks, Lindy stayed at Reggie's side as they walked around the village. Nature was at its best at this time, the grass, the trees and everywhere looked luscious, full of life and were beautiful.

They went on the same bus to school, and parted their ways at the corner of Star Street. Lindy worried about him, and would have loved to be at his side during school hours.

He did however manage to cope with school. But he was very quiet and did what he was asked, but offered little more. He answered questions, and produced work. However, he found it hard to add any enthusiasm to anything he did.

At the end of the day, Lindy rushed out of school to the corner of Star Street, as she wanted to make sure she was in good time to be there waiting for him.

'Nice day?' she enquired.

'Not bad,' was all he could offer. On one occasion he was carrying a rolled-up picture under his arm.

'What's the picture?' asked Lindy.

'It's nothing,' he replied.

'It can't be nothing!' said Lindy. 'Let me see ... please!'

He handed it to her. Lindy unrolled it, and saw that it was yet again another picture of fire, and black silhouettes of people running about. The fire was painted in streaks of brilliant red, with bands of yellow and black running through it. The ground was covered in bricks, rubble and beams from bombed out houses.

'Another picture of the fire,' said Lindy gently. 'Why don't you paint something else?'

He shrugged his shoulders. Lindy said no more, but rolled up the picture and handed it back to him carefully.

The other companion who was always faithfully at Reggie's side was Texi. He somehow sensed Reggie's sorrow and that he needed him. Texi always greeted him with a cheery bark and a wagging tail. Reggie responded and crouched down, stroked his head and patted his back. He was allowed to take him for walks mainly in the grounds of the big house. Texi stayed close to him except when he found a smell that was too interesting to resist.

One day they ended up on the beach. It was late afternoon and the sun was still shining making the sea sparkle. 'It's calm today,' Reggie told Texi. The dog came up to him and together they sat quietly on the sand. Texi's head was on Reggie's lap in the right place so he could be stroked.

The waves lapped the shore in a soft rhythmical sound. The sand looked more golden than ever, and the sky was a beautiful shade of blue.

'This is so lovely Texi,' he said. 'Do you think heaven is like this?'

Out of the corner of his eye, Reggie became aware of a small girl running along the beach in and out of the water. A lady was running behind her.

'Stop Bethany!' said the lady. 'You've got your shoes on!'

The lady ran after her, caught her, picked her up and swung her around. Bethany giggled. The lady put her down on the ground and took off her shoes and socks.

'They are all wet! Oh, Bethany you are a naughty girl. You are going to have to walk home in wet shoes.'

She stood up in bare feet and wiggled her toes in the soft sand. Then she ran off giggling. The lady followed, and caught her again, picking her up and swinging her around in the air. The little girl giggled again. She obviously enjoyed the game.

'What a lovely scene, Texi. I wish I could paint the sea like it is with the sun shining on it, the sky as blue as it is and capture the movement of the little girl being swung in the air.'

Bethany stopped in front of Reggie and Texi. 'Hello,' said Reggie. 'Are you enjoying the beach?'

'Dog!' said Bethany.

'Yes, this is Texi!'

'Dog!' repeated Bethany.

'Do you want to stroke him?' asked Reggie.

Bethany came closer and the lady followed.

'He's alright,' called Reggie. 'He won't hurt you; he is as soft as butter.'

'Alright. Bethany be gentle.' The lady sat down on the soft sand next to Reggie.

Bethany was gentle and copying Reggie's demonstration, she stroked Texi's soft head. She giggled again. 'Dog!' she repeated. 'Dog!'

Texi must have taken Bethany's giggling for a sign to get up and play. He rushed away from the group towards the sea, the toddler followed.

'Bethany!' called the lady.

'I'll get her,' said Reggie.

He chased after her. 'Bethany, come here,' he called. Hearing her name she stopped, turned around and fell backwards and sat on the wet sand. Reggie put his hands under her arms and picked her up. Suddenly he had a recollection of being back in East Cowes. He held Bethany close to him and cradled her head close to his chest. The little girl giggled again, as she wanted to be swung around. Reggie obliged. The two played the game for a while. Bethany ran, Reggie caught her and swung her high in the air. Their laughter could be heard along the beach. Texi barked and wagged his tail as he chased around in the surf.

Exhausted Reggie took Bethany's hand and walked back to where he had been sitting. Lindy was there.

'You were having fun,' said Lindy.

'Yes!' said Reggie slightly exaggerating his exhaustion.

Lindy had been introduced to Susannah at Auntie Bee's house. She had been able to track down the scout who had rescued her daughter from the rubble.

'Susannah,' said Lindy. 'This is Reggie,'

'How do you do?' said Reggie. 'Oh Lindy, you know each other.'

'We have only just met!' said Lindy. 'She came to the cottage looking for you.'

'I am staying with my sister in Church Lane, we were bombed out of our house in East Cowes in May.'

The words East Cowes suddenly made Reggie shudder.

'Bethany,' he said. 'Shall we make a sand castle?' He jumped up found a flat stone and using it like a spade, started to dig and made a heap of sand. Then he collected some shells to put around the creation. The little girl joined in.

'Well Bethany,' said Reggie 'I wouldn't have put that shell there, but then that's where you want the shell to be put, who am I to argue with a fellow artist.'

That's a long sentence, thought Lindy. *All I usually hear from Reggie is short one-word answers.*

They stayed on the beach for quite a time. Bethany enjoyed Reggie's company. Reggie taught her to say 'shell' and 'rock' as they built their castle. She would insist on called Reggie, Reddy.

'It's Reggie,' he said. 'Reg gie'. She looked straight back at him and said Red dy.'

'It's like they have a bond between them,' said Susannah who was putting Bethany's shoes on. 'They are like brother and sister.'

She turned to Reggie, 'I'm told you are a scout! Is that right?'

'Yes, I am,' replied Reggie, who had suddenly to make a dash after Bethany. She was about to go into the sea again wearing her shoes.

'You are the scout that rescued my ...' she called after him. But Susannah's words were lost in the breeze and not heard by Reggie.

Bethany and her mother walked back along the beach to the exit where the path separated around the oak tree. Lindy and Reggie turned and sauntered towards the woods and gardens belonging to the Quays.

'Didn't you understand Reggie?' said Lindy. 'She is the little girl you pulled out of the rubble in East Cowes that day.'

'Yes, I thought I recognised her!' said Reggie. Later he added, 'Then it was alright!'

'Pardon?' said Lindy what do you mean?'

'Bethany! I mean. Bethany is alive and well! So, it's alright, isn't it?' Reggie paused and then he said. 'I wonder what is for supper, I'm starving!

Postscript

Nature can hide a lot of things. Whilst the people from Cowes and East Cowes were busy clearing up after their raid, plants were growing. Oblivious of the war, trees were springing into life and leaves were sprouting from the branches, first appearing in a pale shade of yellow which developed into a luscious green.

There was a hedge opposite Osborne House that was hiding a secret. It too had blossomed into life. The grass in front of it had grown tall. No-one knew that it was hiding a precious secret.

After a stormy night, George and Doris were riding into East Cowes on their Waggonette, when Doris spotted a glint of something shiny in the hedge. The heavy rain had beaten down some of the grass in front of the hedge thus exposing this sparkly object.

'Stop George, oh please stop!' said Doris. 'There is something over there that is glinting in the sunlight.'

George gently tightened the reigns and Sergeant stopped obediently. Doris jumped down, still keeping her eyes of this shining object. The grass was long and wet, she had to lift the skirt of her summer dress to prevent it from becoming damp. Pushing back the grass revealed a set of handle bars. She pulled at it, and out came a bicycle.

'It's a bike!' shouted Doris. Some Columbine had entwined itself around the frame and wheel. Once released from its restraints, Doris tore off the remaining plant growth, pulled it out and held it high.

'It's a child's bike!' said Doris.

'Bring it over here,' said George. 'We'll put it in the back and take it home to keep it safe. I wonder who has lost that?'

'George! George!' said Doris excitedly. 'I know just whose bike this belongs to.'

'Who?'

'I saw Cludgy last week and she told me that on the night of the raid, Reggie rode into East Cowes on a bike. That was Lindy's bike which he borrowed. He fell off and abandoned it in the hedge somewhere near Osborne House. We have found Lindy's bike!'

Doris wrote immediately to Lindy to tell her the good news, and arrangements were made for Doris and George to come over to Little Bridge to have lunch and return the bike.

They decided between them, that Doris and George would bring over some cheese and tomatoes, and Cludgy would provide a green salad, she would also provide some boiled new potatoes from the allotment, and some meat.

I won't know what meat,' wrote Cludgy, 'until nearer the day, as I won't know what would be available.'

Lindy was thrilled to be getting her bike back. She loved it ever since Arthur had cleaned it up and the Reverend Peterson had mended it.

Reggie was making good progress, in the absence of his parents to talk to. He spent many hours talking to Reverend Peterson on the flat grave stone under the yew tree. He let Reggie just talk, and only spoke when necessary. He also spent time with Texi, playing on the beach. When Lindy wasn't busy with her school work, she would join in. She too knew when to speak and when to just say nothing.

At Scouts, he gained his National Service Award. He achieved 76 hours in just four months, well over the amount of hours required. He did a variety of jobs, collecting salvage, gardening, and helping move furniture on to a lorry, when an old lady had to move from her bomb-damaged house.

His favourite job was to help the milkman who had a horse and half waggonette to carry his milk around the area. In May after the East Cowes bombing, he had been asleep when he had a lift home with George and Doris. Consequently, he didn't know the story about Queen Victoria's half waggonette that George related. Lindy told him. After that he was always careful where he put the milk in the back. The padded benches had been covered to protect them; a board had been put across to enable more milk to be carried. This made it a little difficult to imagine Queen Victoria seated in the back.

An important scout leader came to present him with his award. 'What was his name?' asked Auntie Bee, Lindy,

Arthur and Cludgy. 'I don't know, I was told, but I have forgotten.'

Lindy's main worry after the raid was Clarissa and her mother. She did not know where they were, or whether they survived the raid.

She scoured the local papers, asked her father to make enquiries, and even asked Reverend Mother if she had any news. It was a relief for her to discover that they were not on the list of the dead or injured.

Lindy was haunted by how she became separated from them on the night of the raid.

'I was running, and I thought they were running too, I fell down to the ground when another bomb was dropped, and when I got up afterwards,' she said, 'They weren't there.'

Lindy's concerns finally reached the manager at Whites where Clarissa's father worked. He in turn passed on the information to the ARP warden in East Cowes. He had heard that Lindy had been looking for Clarissa and wrote to Arthur. Consequently, it was after a full fortnight before she discovered just what had happened to them. They too told the same story of running and dropping down to the ground, but they had been running in an opposite direction to Lindy. Their house was badly damaged, but Lindy's school bag was rescued and was in the safe hands of the ARP warden, who said he would get it back to her.

Clarissa and her mother were quite shaken by the raid, and her father was given time off to take them to Cornwall to stay with Muriel's sister.

Bethany's mother often used the pretty bay at Little Bridge as a place for her to play. They frequently met up with Reggie and Lindy who too used the bay for relaxing. They had grown quite tall; Reggie now was taller of the two.

He now no longer raced at top speed around the village from one place to another. He was more measured in his actions, gave more thought to what he was doing. His work at school was improving, his art work was developing, and he began to enjoy mathematics because it related to what he was making in wood work. He was very speedy however when he was playing football or chasing Bethany on the beach.

Lindy continued to work steadily at the convent. She remained in contact by letter with Clarissa telling her all the news from school. The bullies no longer had any hold over the class having been exposed. Anything nasty that was said was just ignored; they got bored and gave up. History lessons continued to be boring, until she found pictures of Henry VIII and his six wives in an encyclopaedia in a box of books stored in her bedroom. Cludgy told her the stories of each of the women, and Lindy was then interested.

'Oh, Cludgy thank you. Why can't you be our history teacher?'

The friendship of the two evacuees was stronger than ever. The two had encountered the terrifying and horrid side of war. Reggie had been incredibly brave rescuing Bethany from under the rubble, and Lindy had found a new strength getting Reggie to safety on that awful night.

There were prayers for peace said at both of their schools and at church.

'Oh, but when will it come?' said Reggie as they sat together on Little Bridge beach.

'I don't know,' said Lindy. 'I wish it would come soon.'

The sky was a beautiful rich blue that only comes when the sun is shining very brightly.

'Wouldn't it be lovely to sit here,' said Reggie, 'Without worrying about the siren being sounded.'

'One day,' said Lindy. She sighed. 'There will be blue skies without war.'

This is Jo's third book about Lindy and Reggie's adventures in Little Bridge on the Isle of Wight. The first one, 'A Red Sky' was awarded third place in the Isle of Wight Book Awards, Children's section, for books published in 2022.

'A Red Sky' and 'Sparkles in the Navy-Blue Sky' are still available from Amazon or from Jo directly via her website.

jo@jocooperbooks.com

Printed in Great Britain
by Amazon